THE
BYZANTINE THEOCRACY

THE WEIL LECTURES
CINCINNATI 1973

THE
BYZANTINE THEOCRACY

STEVEN RUNCIMAN

CAMBRIDGE UNIVERSITY PRESS

CAMBRIDGE

LONDON · NEW YORK · MELBOURNE

Published by the Syndics of the Cambridge University Press
The Pitt Building, Trumpington Street, Cambridge CB2 IRP
Bentley House, 200 Euston Road, London NW1 2DB
32 East 57th Street, New York, NY 10022, USA
296 Beaconsfield Parade, Middle Park, Melbourne 3206, Australia

© Cambridge University Press 1977

First published 1977

Printed in Great Britain
at the
University Press, Cambridge

Library of Congress Cataloguing in Publication Data
Runciman, Steven, Sir, 1903–
The Byzantine theocracy.

(The Weil lectures; 1973)
Includes bibliographical references and index.
1. Church and state in the Byzantine Empire—
History—Addresses, essays, lectures. I. Title.
II. Series.
BX300.R86   274.95   76–47405
ISBN 0 521 21401 7

CONTENTS

CONTENTS

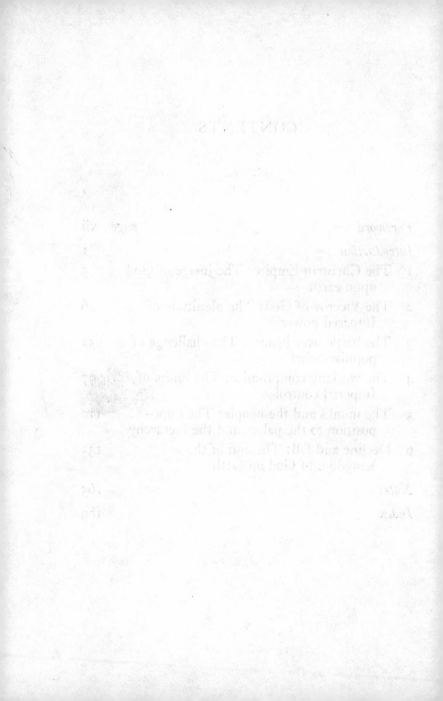

FOREWORD

In the autumn of 1973 I was invited by the Weil Institute of Cincinnati to give a series of lectures there on the subject of Church and State in Byzantium. It was an invitation and an assignment for which I was deeply grateful, not only because of the generous hospitality that I received in Cincinnati, but also because it enabled me to order my thoughts on a fundamental question in Byzantine history.

The six lectures that I gave to the Institute are reproduced here, with a few minor adjustments, needed when the spoken word is transformed into the written word, and with the addition of reference notes. In a short book which covers so wide a subject it would be impractical to attempt to give the original sources for every fact and episode mentioned in the book. I have given the sources for direct quotations; but in general I have referred to modern works in which the interested reader can find further information and bibliographical material on any topic into which he may wish to go further. The references that I give will also indicate how much I am indebted to various scholars whose works have illuminated for me various aspects of the subject.

There is always a problem in the transliteration of proper names from the Greek. A completely consistent system is, I think, impossible without a pedantic introduction of ridiculously unfamiliar forms. I have simply employed in every case what seems to me to be the most familiar form.

INTRODUCTION

The aim of this short study is to give an account of
an Empire whose constitution, to use too legal a
word, was based on a clear religious conviction: that
it was the earthly copy of the Kingdom of Heaven.
Many tribes and nations have seen themselves as
being the favoured children of God or His special
elect. Wherever monarchy has been established the
monarch was always in the beginning either an
emanation of God or a descendant of God, or at
least His High Priest, the man appointed by God to
look after the people. But the Empire which we call
for convenience Byzantine maintained a larger conception. It saw itself as a universal Empire. Ideally
it should embrace all the peoples of the earth, who,
ideally, should all be members of the one true
Christian Church, its own Orthodox Church. Just as
man was made in God's image, so man's kingdom
on earth was made in the image of the Kingdom of
Heaven. Just as God ruled in Heaven, so an Emperor,
made in His image, should rule on earth and carry
out His commandments. Evil had made its way into

God's creation, and man was stained with sin. But if the copy – the Greek word was *mimesis*, 'imitation' – could be achieved, with the Emperor and his ministers and counsellors imitating God with His archangels and angels and saints, then life on earth could become a proper preparation for the truer reality of life in Heaven. The Byzantine Empire lasted for eleven centuries, most of them centuries of decline: till in the end the Emperor ruled over little more than a decayed city-state. Sin had triumphed, and God was punishing the earthly Empire for its failure to copy the divine example. Yet, to the last, the Emperor remained in Byzantine eyes the Viceroy of God, the sacred head of the peoples of the earth.

It was a conception that had no exact parallel. The Holy Roman Empire of the West which, as Voltaire pointed out long ago, was neither holy nor Roman nor an empire, vaguely held the same idea of the Emperor's divine vice-royalty; but it was too deeply involved in feudal and racial traditions to implement the idea; and the Western Emperor had an abler rival in the Roman pontiff: who, in his turn, was limited by his priesthood. The Muslim Caliph was perhaps a closer parallel; for Islam was ideally a universal faith, and the Commander of the Faithful was its priest-king. But Islamic thought did not see him as the Viceroy of God. Even the Prophet himself had only been the Prophet of God. The Caliph was not the earthly imitation of God but, rather, his inspired Prime Minister.

The theory was clear and simple. The practice was more complicated. The Byzantine Empire was in fact the Roman Empire. Constantine the Great had given it a new character by moving its capital to the East and by converting it into a Christian Empire. But it could not shed its Roman past. In particular, it could not forget Roman Law, which was essentially a secular law, a law evolved by a race of practical administrators, which had now become a deeply respected basis of society. What were to be the relations of the Viceroy of God with this pre-Christian instrument of government? Then again, the Roman Empire, especially its eastern half, in which the new capital of Constantinople was placed, was proudly conscious of ancient Greek culture, of Greek philosophy and the Greek science of politics. Could this consciousness be shed? The new faith might be able to curtail philosophical speculation; but could it eliminate Greek words such as 'tyranny', 'oligarchy' and 'democracy'? The adoption of the new religion itself posed a further problem. An institutional religion has to have its hierarchy of priests, both the men who are trained and ordained to conduct the religious services and the upper hierarchs whose business it is to organize the machinery of religion. Would the priests and hierarchs accept the orders of a Viceroy of God when it was their own duty to interpret the teachings of God and to arrange for His worship? These were the problems that were bound to affect in practice the theory of Byzantine theocracy; and at their head was the problem of the relations of what are usually called Church and State.

A cautious comment must here be inserted about the word 'Church'. To the Christians of the East the Greek word *ecclesia*, or 'church', has always meant the whole body of the faithful, alive and dead. This is the Church mentioned in the Creed. But in practice, especially in the West, we use the word 'Church' more and more to describe the priestly hierarchy, as opposed to the lay authorities. Indeed, owing to the deficiency of the English language, there is no other suitable word for the hierarchy. But in contrasting Church with State we are making a distinction which would have been meaningless to the Byzantines; and in making it we are committing a historical and a philological error. It was, in fact, the lack of this distinction which caused its chief problem to the Byzantine theocracy.

1

THE CHRISTIAN EMPIRE:
THE IMAGE OF GOD UPON EARTH

Whether or not it was granted to the Emperor Constantine to experience a vision which turned him to support the Christian Faith is a question about which historians will always argue according to their tastes. His biographer Eusebius relates that the Emperor many years later told him, rather shyly, that on his way to invade Italy in A.D. 312 he had a sudden vision of a cross shining against the midday sun, and below it the words: 'In this, conquer.' That night Christ came to him in a dream and bade him place upon the shields of his troops the *labarum*, the Christian monogram XP.[1] Rationalist historians dismiss the tale as being the invention of Constantine himself, or, more probably, of Eusebius, whom they dismiss as an unreliable sycophant. Pious Christians see in it a miracle. Others believe that Constantine saw a rare but not unique natural phenomenon which he exaggerated in his imagination. That his soldiers wore the monogram at the battle of the Milvian Bridge a few weeks later is testified by the historian Lactantius, who, however, says that Constantine's inspiration was given to him on the eve of the battle.[2] The stories are not necessarily contradictory. Constantine was talking to Eusebius twenty-six years after the event, and he may genuinely have forgotten the time-lag between his two visionary experiences. It is well attested that when he entered Rome as a victor at the end of October 312, his troops had a Christian symbol as their standard; and they carried the standard with them on the campaigns in the East that made Constantine the master of the world.[3]

It has been the general fashion amongst historians to depict Constantine as a shrewd and sceptical politician who saw that an alliance with the Christians would benefit the Imperial cause. That view is, I think, based upon hindsight. The Roman Empire was certainly beset with problems, constitutional and military, social and economic, all of which created and were increased by an atmosphere of hopelessness and fear. Thoughtful Emperors had long sought for a moral force that would unite and inspire their subjects. The persecution of definite sects such as the Christians had been part of a policy that aimed at moral unity. If the Emperors had leaned towards a cult such as that of the Undying Sun, they had never intended the cult to be exclusive. It was to be the basis of a new syncretism. To patronize the Christians whose religion was essentially exclusive was a revolution in policy. It was also a risky gamble. It has been calculated that at the time of the Edict of Milan in 313, when the Christian Church was given complete freedom of worship and a legal status, the Christians did not number more than a seventh of the population of the Empire. The Christians were, moreover, very poorly represented in the army, which was the Emperor's main source of power. Constantine may have hopefully believed that his own devotion to the Sun could be combined with Christianity; for Christian writers had often used the sun as a symbol of the undying light of God. It is true that the Christians were the best organized of the religious sects within the Empire, and that their leaders included many of its ablest citizens. But at that moment, as Constantine soon discovered, if he did not know it already, they were divided by schism and heresy, which lessened their potential strength. It is hard to believe that he would have taken the risk of identifying himself with them, even though he in no way removed toleration from the pagans, had his conversion not been sincere so far as it went. His subsequent words and actions show that he took his patronage of Christianity very seriously. If by so doing he managed to enhance the power of the Imperial autocracy, this was due more to circumstances and to the wishes and the failings of the Christians than to any far-sighted calculation on his part.[4]

So long as the Christians formed a minority group without legal recognition it was impossible for them to enforce theological uniformity or ecclesiastical discipline. They could not control heresy, when there was no clear official orthodoxy, nor prevent schism, when there were no legal sanctions for their administration. As far as was possible they were effectively organized. Each local church was under the complete authority of its bishop, elected for life by the clergy and representatives of the laity of the see, with the consent of the neighbouring bishops, one of whom would consecrate him, so that the apostolic succession from Christ's disciples would be maintained. The charismatic equality of all bishops has never been challenged in Eastern Christendom; but in the latter part of the third century, in the period between the persecutions of Valerian and of Diocletian, when the number of Christians rose sharply, it became the custom of bishops to meet now and then in conclave in the local metropolis, under the presidency of the metropolitan bishop, who thus gradually obtained an undefined administrative and even spiritual authority over his fellows. For the sake of convenience the ecclesiastical pattern followed geographically that of the lay government; and when Diocletian grouped the provinces into vast dioceses, the bishops of the great cities in which the Prefects resided acquired a practical authority over the metropolitans of the provincial centres. By the early fourth century three bishops had moved ahead of the others. The bishop of Rome was already considered to have a certain primacy over all other bishops, because Rome was the Imperial capital and the city in which Saint Peter and Saint Paul had been martyred, and because the first bishop of Rome had been, according to tradition, Saint Peter, the chief of the apostles. The bishop of Antioch was held to be head of all the bishops in the Asiatic provinces of the Empire; and his see also had been founded by Saint Peter. The bishop of Alexandria, though his see had only been founded by Saint Mark and his territory was restricted to Egypt, was in practical power the most formidable of the three. Alexandria was the intellectual centre of the Empire. The teeming population of Egypt was almost entirely Christian, probably outnumbering the Christian population in either Europe or Asia; and the bishop, copying the example of the lay governor of Egypt, who, until Diocletian's reforms, had enjoyed full vice-regal powers, had established the right himself to appoint every bishop within the diocese. A little behind these three came the bishop of Carthage, whose province of Africa also contained a thick concentration of Christians, but who was fighting a losing battle to keep himself independent of Rome.[5]

These great hierarchs each tried to maintain discipline and a conformity of belief in his area; and, so far as mutual jealousy allowed, they kept in touch with each other on matters of policy and doctrine. It was not easy, as they had no weapon other than excommunication; and many doctrines were still un-defined. The two greatest Christian Fathers of the pre-Constantinian age, Origen of Alexandria in the East and Tertullian of Carthage in the West, had both lapsed from generally accepted orthodoxy; and though neither therefore received the accolade of canonization, both had a profound influence on theology. The Gnostic sects had indeed been ejected from the Church. But that was chiefly because they had no wish to remain within it. Other disputes and dissensions could not be so easily solved.

Constantine had barely given the Christians their freedom of worship before he found himself involved in their quarrels. Controversies were raging both in Egypt and in Africa, both originating from the same problem. During the persecutions a number of Christians, priests as well as laymen, submitted to the pagan authorities. Were they to be re-admitted to the Church? Already after Decius's persecution a Roman priest, Novatian, had led a party that refused to communicate with back-sliders, however repentant; and the Novatianists were not extinct.[6] During Dio-cletian's persecution an altercation had arisen between two Egyptian bishops, Peter of Alexandria and Melitius of Lycopolis, when Peter proposed light penalties for believers who had sacrificed at the pagan altars, scaled according to whether they had been threatened death, torture or merely imprisonment. When Peter on his release carried out his programme,

Melitius and his friends would not co-operate; and when Peter was re-arrested and martyred in 312 the Melitians would not recognize his successor, Alexander.[7] In Africa at the same time the pagan authorities had insisted on the sacred books of the Christians being handed over to them. A number of bishops obeyed, to save their congregations; but an extremist party would have nothing more to do with them. When in 311 a new Bishop of Carthage, Caecilian, was elected, these extremists – supported by the funds of a rich lady, Lucilla, who personally disliked Caecilian – challenged the election because he had been consecrated by Felix of Aptunga, a bishop who had been one of the *traditores*, the handers-over of books. Instead, they elected a certain Majorinus, who died a few months later and was succeeded by Donatus, who gave his name to the party.[8]

The Melitians were confined to Egypt; and several years passed before the Emperor became aware of them. But he had only been a few months in Rome before the Donatist schism was brought to his notice. Miltiades, Bishop of Rome, an African by birth, was deeply worried by the schism, as was the Bishop of Cordova, Hosius, whom Constantine had taken as his spiritual adviser. Hosius recommended that the Emperor give his patronage to Caecilian. Thereupon the Donatists sent an appeal to the Emperor, a gesture that was all the more remarkable as they do not seem to have realized that he was already a Christian.

Constantine thus found himself invited to be the arbiter on a wholly ecclesiastical dispute. He responded readily to the invitation. In a letter to Miltiades, in which he said that it was intolerable that the people of a province which divine providence had entrusted to his care should be divided into two camps, he told the Bishop of Rome to preside over a commission with three bishops from Gaul (the Donatists having asked for Gallic bishops, as being impartial), which would interview ten African bishops from each party. Such a commission represented a Roman civilian's method for dealing with disputes of that type. Miltiades deftly turned it into a Church Council by adding fourteen Italian bishops to the tribunal. Constantine took the point. When the Donatists refused to accept the decisions of this Council, he summoned a Council of all the bishops of the West to hear the case, to meet at Arles in 314.[9]

Whatever Miltiades might think, it was Constantine who summoned the Council of Arles and who considered it his duty to do so. Though he tolerated pagan cults, he was genuinely distressed by schism in the Church and felt personally responsible for restoring unity. In his letter to the Prefect of Africa ordering him to send the African bishops to Arles he wrote: 'I consider it to be by no means right that such altercations should be hidden from me, owing to which God may perhaps be moved not only against the human race but also against myself, to whom by His divine decree He has entrusted the direction of all human affairs.'[10] The Council of Arles rejected the Donatists' case; and they refused to accept its findings. Thereupon Constantine wrote to the assembled bishops before they left Arles to express his anger and to repeat that he would regard it as his Imperial duty to see that the schismatics were punished.[11] In 316 he finally gave judgment in favour of Caecilian.[12]

With the Donatists the problem was that of schism; for no one touched upon the underlying theological question: was the grace bestowed upon a bishop at his consecration annulled if he committed mortal sin? It was not long, however, before Constantine was faced with a problem that involved fundamental Christian theology. By the end of 324, fighting as a Christian champion, he had defeated his co-Emperor Licinius and became sole autocrat of the Empire. But hardly had he arrived in the East and settled himself in Nicomedia, then the administrative capital of the East, than he learnt that the Eastern Church was split on a matter of doctrine.

This is not the place in which to give a detailed discussion of Arianism. But some basic facts must be remembered. Arius was an Alexandrian priest with a talent for preaching who in about 319 promulgated a doctrine that Christ was not eternal but had been created by God as an instrument for the creation and redemption of the world. He was the Son of God, but not of the same nature as God the Father. It was not an entirely new doctrine. It derived partly from the Neoplatonic idea of the monad and partly from Jewish tradition, and in the milder form of Sub-ordinationism – that is, the placing of the Son in a subordinate position to the Father – had been implicitly held by such Fathers of the Church as Justin, Irenaeus and Clement of Alexandria, and more explicitly by Origen; and Lucian of Antioch, a sainted martyr who had been Arius's teacher, seems openly to have preached it. Arius merely gave the doctrine a more precise and more easily intelligible form. For this he was excommunicated by a Council of Egyptian bishops summoned by the Bishop of Alexandria, Alexander. But Arius kept many followers in Egypt, especially among women. He was usually accompanied, we are told, by 700 holy and vociferous virgins. He found supporters too in Asia. At his request Eusebius, Bishop of Nicomedia, who had studied with him under Lucian, summoned a Council of bishops in his province of Bithynia, which endorsed the Arian doctrine. Arius then went to Palestine, where Eusebius, Bishop of Caesarea, showed himself to be sympathetic. A Council of Palestinian bishops also approved his doctrine but urged him to seek reconciliation with Alexander of Alexandria. Alexander, who was a peaceable man, hoped that Arius would calm down and let the controversy lapse. But Arius was now too powerfully supported to remain silent. There followed a war of pamphlets, more and more bitter in tone, with mutual accusations of heresy.[13]

Constantine was horrified to find the East as fiercely divided as Africa had been, over what seemed to him to be a trifling matter. He wrote a letter which he ordered Hosius of Cordova to take to Egypt, to show to both Alexander and Arius. Let them copy the philosophers, he wrote, who if they disagree on one little point still co-operate to maintain the unity of philosophical doctrine. He wished himself to visit Egypt but could not do so in face of such quarrels. 'Open to me by your agreement the road to the East, which you have closed by your discord.'[14]

Hosius found neither Arius nor Alexander tractable, and he also learnt about the Melitian schism. He advised the Emperor to take action. Meanwhile a rabid anti-Arian, Marcellus, Bishop of Ankyra decided to hold a council of local bishops to denounce Arius, while, in conjunction, the Syrian bishops, assembled at Antioch to elect its new bishop, not only chose another fierce anti-Arian, Eustathius, but also condemned three bishops, including Eusebius of Caesarea, for Arian tendencies. Constantine was not pleased; but he outwitted Marcellus by taking the council to be held at Ankyra under his own patronage, enlarging it and moving it to Nicaea, to which city he summoned all the bishops of Christendom.[15]

The Council of Nicaea, the First Oecumenical Council, was a pivotal event in the history of

Christianity. But in fact we know very little about it. Probably some five hundred bishops attended, nearly all from the Greek-speaking East, about one hundred of them from Asia Minor. The West was not much interested. The Bishop of Rome, Sylvester, pleaded ill health and sent two deacons to represent him. Only one bishop came from Italy, one from Gaul and one from Illyricum. Caecilian of Carthage was there, but no one from Britain nor from Spain, except for Hosius of Cordova, who attended as the Emperor's deputy. Five bishops came from beyond the eastern frontier of the Empire.[16] The Council was formally opened on 20 May 325. When the bishops were all assembled the Emperor entered wearing his purple Imperial robes; but he modestly refused to be seated till the bishops gave him permission. After he had been formally welcomed by the bishop seated on his right – probably Eustathius of Antioch, but the name is not given – he made a short speech, in Latin, followed by a Greek translation, in which he deplored the quarrels within the Church and urged the bishops to win the favour of God and the gratitude of the Emperor by composing their discord. It is uncertain how often he appeared at subsequent debates and how far he left Hosius in charge.[17] The course of the debates is equally uncertain. We know that Eusebius of Caesarea, no doubt at the request of the Emperor, who approved of him as a moderate, proposed that the Council should endorse the traditional Creed of the church of Caesarea. Its wording about Christ was impeccably Orthodox, but it contained nothing that might offend the Arians. The bishops could not but accept it; but the anti-Arians insisted that some stronger clause should be added.[18] As the debates became more acrimonious Constantine intervened with the suggestion that the word *homoousios*, 'of the same essence', should be inserted to describe the Son's relation to the Father. The word was not new to theology. It had been condemned by an Eastern Council in 268. But Rome regarded it as Orthodox; and it was doubtless Hosius who, being a Westerner and ignorant of its history in the East, recommended it to the Emperor.[19] Both parties in the East disliked it, but they were cowed by the presence of the Emperor, though the anti-Arians added two or three explanatory phrases.[20] When the vote was taken on the formula only two bishops refused assent. They, along with Arius, were then excommunicated. At the same time the Melitian schism was ended with a compromise. The Melitian bishops were to be regarded as being properly consecrated if they submitted to the authority of Alexander of Alexandria. It seemed that the Melitians were anti-Arian and therefore ripe for reconciliation.[21]

Constantine was delighted by the outcome of the Council. 'At the suggestion of God', he wrote to the Church of Alexandria, 'I assembled at Nicaea a vast number of bishops, with whom I, as one, very glad to be your fellow-servant, undertook myself the examination of the truth.'[22] His delight was not justified in the short view. Arius would not be silenced; and while Alexander of Alexandria was ready to be conciliatory, his successor, Athanasius, was of sterner stuff. His intransigence soon brought him into conflict with the Emperor, who now inclined towards a mildly Subordinationist theology, probably inspired by Eusebius of Caesarea, who seems to have succeeded the aging Hosius as his chief spiritual adviser. Constantine's mother, Helena, had a devoted veneration for Lucian of Antioch, Arius's teacher, to whom she dedicated a great church in the city of Helenopolis, which she founded. Eustathius of Antioch therefore disliked her and spread unkind stories about her early life. He was promptly deposed, allegedly for immorality. Another rabid anti-Arian, Marcellus of Ankyra, was deposed for having made a fool of himself in a dispute with Eusebius of Nicomedia and Eusebius of Caesarea, both of whom had the Emperor's ear. Even Athanasius was ultimately suspended from his see and sent into temporary exile. Constantine had planned to bring unity to the Church. It remained as divided as ever.[23]

It is hardly surprising that the Emperor became angrier and more autocratic. We find him, when arranging for a Council to be held at Tyre in 335, writing in his circular to the bishops that: 'If anyone should ignore my summons, which I do not expect,

I shall send someone who at my command will drive him out and teach him that he has no right to resist the Emperor's orders issued in defence of the truth.'[24] We find him writing to the heretics that their foul behaviour justifies Imperial intervention and punishment. He called himself 'bishop of those outside of the Church', by which he seems to have meant that he was responsible for the souls of pagans, whom he was prepared to tolerate, and heretics, whom he would not tolerate.[25] He also, as a letter to the King of Persia shows, felt himself to be responsible for Christians living beyond his frontiers.[26] Yet he was modest. He knew that it was for the bishops in council, not for himself, to pronounce on theological and even on ecclesiastical problems, although he might, as at Nicaea, rather forcibly suggest the solution. It was probably diffidence that made him postpone his baptism till his death-bed, when he was baptized by the semi-Arian, Eusebius of Nicomedia. But he earnestly believed that it was his holy duty as Emperor to see that the Church to which he had been converted was united and strong; and by this conviction he set the pattern for the future.

How could the Church accept this new master? Hitherto it had been autonomous. It had always tried to obey Christ's injunction to render unto Caesar the things which were his. It had listened to Saint Paul's command to honour the king. Saint Athenagoras of Athens had been quite ready to flatter Marcus Aurelius by pronouncing him as excelling all men not only in power and intelligence but in an accurate knowledge of all learning.[27] Tertullian emphasized the loyalty of Christians to the Emperor. 'We are always praying for him', he says. 'We must respect him as the chosen of God. I can even say that he is more ours than the pagans', as he was appointed by our God.'[28] The Christians wished to be good citizens, obedient to the lay authorities. If the emperor became Christian, surely any tension between the Imperial government and the Church would cease. But did the Victory of the Cross give the Emperor any rights over the religious life of the Christians?

The notion of the priest-king is to be found in the Old Testament, with the shadowy figure of Melchisedec, and later with David; and there was Moses who had led the people and who had personally received the Commandments of God, even though Aaron was the official High Priest. A ruler with a special relationship with God was thus not unknown to the Jews and therefore to the early Christians.[29] It was, however, in Persia that the idea of the divine monarch was developed. There, as far back as pre-Zoroastrian times, the King was the possessor of the *hvarena*, an awe-inspiring glory that was given to him by the God of Light. It was symbolized by the halo, and, more materially, by the shining diadem and the shimmering robes that a king should wear.[30] Even earlier, the Egyptians had stressed the divine origin of the monarchy; but there the power of the priesthood seems to have kept monarchical ambitions in check.[31] Many Persian and Egyptian notions came into Greek philosophy. We find Aristotle declaring the ideal king to be the earthly image of Zeus, and Isocrates that he is the earthly image of Heracles.[32] But it was in the Hellenistic kingdoms, whose monarchs saw themselves as being divine after the Persian model, that the philosophy of kingship was developed. In the sixth century A.D. a certain John Stobaeus published an anthology of essays on kingship which he blithely attributed to a number of ancient philosophers, but which all seem actually to date from the third and second centuries B.C. In it 'Archytas' declares that the king is animate law. 'Sthenidas' declares that the wise king is the imitation and the representative of God. 'Diotogenes' declares that as God is in the universe so the king is in the state, and he adds that the state is an imitation of the order and the harmony of the universe, and that the king is transformed into a god among men. Still more significantly, 'Ecphantos' says that the *logos* of God, which sows the seeds of order and visits man to restore what has been lost by sin, is incarnate in the king.[33] Some time later Plutarch takes this up. He says that God has set up as His image in Heaven the sun and the moon, and in earthly polities a similar copy and radiance, the king, who should have as his guiding principle the *logos*.[34]

Constantine was lucky in having as his biographer and panegyrist Eusebius of Caesarea, a scholar who was certainly aware of these texts and who made them the basis of his philosophy of the Christian Empire. First he had to justify the Roman Empire. Philo had shown that Rome had brought peace and unity to the world and thus was favoured of God. Origen had added a Christian argument, showing that God had chosen to send His Son into the world at a moment when Rome had brought this unity and peace, so that the Gospel could travel without hindrance to all people.[35] According to Eusebius the triumph of history had now come, when the Roman Emperor had accepted the Christian message. He was now the wise king who was the imitation of God, ruling a realm which could now become the imitation of Heaven. Eusebius simply adopted the doctrines of Diotogenes, Ecphantus and Plutarch, with suitable modifications. The king is not God among men but the Viceroy of God. He is not the *logos* incarnate but is in a special relation with the *logos*. He has been specially appointed and is continually inspired by God, the friend of God, the interpreter of the Word of God. His eyes look upward, to receive the messages of God. He must be surrounded with the reverence and glory that befits God's earthly copy; and he will 'frame his earthly government according to the pattern of the divine original, finding strength in its conformity with the monarchy of God'.[36]

It was a splendid ideal; but it left many questions unanswered. What were to be the relations of the divine Empire with Roman Law and Roman constitutional traditions? Eusebius was a Hellenized Syrian who knew little of Roman ways. According to Roman theory the Emperor's power was derived from the semi-fictitious *lex de imperio*, by which the Roman People had handed over its sovereign rights to Augustus. He was elected by the Army, the Senate and the People; and were he incompetent or unpopular the electors would see to his fall, either through a revolt in the army, an intrigue in the civil service or a popular riot. Could the holy Viceroy of God be so treated, even though his follies or his sins unfitted him for the role? The new theory ignored the problem. So, in the event, the old practice lasted on. Amongst Constantine's successors, as amongst his predecessors, there were many who met their fate through one of the same three operations. Again, though in Rome the Emperor had already become the source of law, yet the Law itself was greater than he. The new theory, even though it suggested that the Emperor was incarnate Law, could not abolish the sanctity of the Law itself. It was something that even the Emperor must obey. Byzantine jurists were to worry over this problem for centuries to come. Then there was the problem introduced by the triumph of Christianity. How did the priestly hierarchy fit into the theory? Could it tolerate an Emperor who had, to use a modern phrase, a private line to God? Constantine himself admitted that only a Council of bishops could pronounce on theological affairs. But it was for him, he thought, to summon the Council; with his special relationship to God, he could guide it and dominate it. He was fortunate because in his time the Church longed for a ruler who would bring it unity and peace, and because there was no outstanding personality amongst the hierarchs until we come to Athanasius. It is significant that Eusebius was Subordinationist in his theology of the Trinity. It was easy for him to stretch his Subordinationism to include the Emperor as a sort of earthly emanation of the Trinity.[37] Athanasius and his school, with their precise Trinitarian doctrine, could never assent to that. The great hierarchs had tried to be good citizens; but hitherto they had controlled the Church. How could a man like Athanasius, brought up in such a tradition, stomach lay interference, especially if he doubted the strict orthodoxy of the lay authority? There was to be trouble in the future.

Yet, by and large, the Eusebian constitution survived in Byzantium down the centuries. It was never a legal constitution, so it could be adapted to suit the needs of the time. Roman traditions lasted on to temper it and to remind the Emperor that while he represented God before the people, it was his duty also to represent the people before God. It never took root in the West, where it faded out when the practical power of the Empire declined. Western thought preferred the rival conception of Saint Augustine's City of God. But to Byzantium it gave a sense of unity, of self-respect and of divine purpose that sustained the Empire to the last. And the credit for that must go to Constantine, a man who was not remarkable either for intellect or for saintliness, but a practical, tolerant and conscientious administrator who had been genuinely converted to the faith of Christ. Though it was only on his death-bed that he was baptized, and then by a bishop of doubtful orthodoxy, he became one of the most revered of Christian saints, hailed down the centuries as the Peer of the Apostles.

2

THE VICEROY OF GOD:
THE PLENITUDE OF IMPERIAL
POWER

Constantine died, clad in stainless white, on 22 May 337. His dominion passed to his three sons, Constantius, Constantine II and Constans. They divided it between them, Constantine taking the Gauls, Britain and Spain, Constans Italy, Africa and Illyricum, and Constantius the whole of the East. The theory that one God in Heaven should be reflected by one Emperor on earth seemed thus to be abandoned: unless one took a Trinitarian view that they represented the Trinity. This hardly represented their own opinions, for they had been brought up with Arian, or, rather, Subordinationist, sympathies; and each wished his brothers to be subordinated to himself. But Constantine II was killed in 340, when fighting against Constans; and Constans was killed by an usurper, Maxentius, in 350. Maxentius was killed by Constantius in 353. Thenceforward, till he died in 361, with his cousin Julian in revolt against him, Constantius was master of the Empire.[1]

Constantius has been unkindly treated by historians, partly because undue sympathy has been given to

Julian, who hated him, and partly because he offended that great stalwart of Trinitarian Orthodoxy, Athanasius. In fact he was a competent and conscientious ruler, with mildly Arian sympathies, but tolerant and, like his father, anxious to force some acceptable compromise on the Church. His brother Constans, living in the West, came to accept Nicene theology and in 343 summoned a Council to Sardica (Sofia), which upheld the Nicene decrees but which was boycotted by the Eastern bishops.[2] Constantius himself held a number of Councils, which were intended to conciliate the Arians and which were therefore regarded with deep disapproval by Athanasius. Constantius probably did not have the tact and certainly did not have the prestige of his father. Constantine's old friend, Hosius of Cordova, wrote sternly to him: 'Do not meddle in Church affairs nor give orders on them. Rather take instruction from us', adding that 'as we are not permitted to govern the world, so you are not permitted to swing the censer'.[3] Athanasius in his *History of the Arians* compared the Emperor with Ahab, with Belshazzar, and with the Pharaohs. He was a parricide, worse than Pilate, a forerunner of Antichrist. It should be remembered that the *History of the Arians* was intended for private circulation only, and Athanasius asked for all copies to be returned to him. But his language showed that he was not prepared to accept a Viceroy of God who did not share his own views.[4]

Athanasius might have been less intolerant of
Constantius had he foreseen that the next Emperor
would not be a Christian of any sort. Julian's neo-
paganism, with its contemptuous tolerance of Christianity, roused him to wilder fury; it was even more
disturbing for Christians who had come to believe
that the Emperor was the Viceroy of God. But
Julian's experiment was out-of-date and short-lived.
Even if he had not been murdered he could never
have forced his fantastic beliefs on an Empire that
was now predominantly Christian. Half a century of
Imperial patronage had produced a vast increase in
the number of Christian believers. It was too late for
a return to paganism.[5] But Athanasius was little better
satisfied by the Christian Emperors that followed
Julian. Jovian's reign was too short to leave any
mark. His successor, Valentinian, who came from the
West where Arianism was rare, followed a creed of
which Athanasius approved; but he appointed his
brother Valens, who had been won over by the
Arians, as Emperor of the East. Athanasius was
officially in disfavour when he died in 373. But the
force of his personality and the vigour of his writings
saw to it that his doctrines ultimately triumphed –
although their triumph was due to Imperial power.
His strictures against the Emperors were carefully
forgotten.[6]

The Arian Emperor Valens was killed by the
Goths in 378, in the disastrous battle of Adrianople.

His death delighted such Orthodox saints as Ambrose of Milan. His Western colleague, Gratian, Valentinian's successor, was Orthodox; and he handed the Eastern Empire to another Westerner, the Spaniard Theodosius, who shared his religious views. Theodosius was determined to establish religious unity. A decree issued from Thessalonica early in 380 ordered all Christians to follow the Nicene doctrine, 'committed by the apostle Peter to the Romans and now professed by Damasus of Rome and Peter of Alexandria'.[7] Later that year Theodosius entered Constantinople. The mob there had Arian sympathies; but he was not deterred. In May 381, on his summons, a great Council of the Church met in Constantinople. It is known as the Second Oecumenical Council, though in fact no bishop from west of the Adriatic was present, the Bishop of Rome being represented by the Metropolitan of Thessalonica. The Council confirmed the creed and doctrine of Nicaea and anathematized all who would not subscribe to it. The Emperor endorsed the canons and issued laws against those who rejected them.[8] His firmness was successful. Henceforward, though Arianism lingered on in parts of Asia, its power was spent: except amongst the Goths and their fellow tribes. They had been converted to Christianity by Bishop Ulfilas, a Goth who was the disciple of Eusebius of Nicomedia; and their obstinate Arianism was to trouble the Western Church greatly during the next two centuries.[9]

The decline of Arianism in the East was helped by the three Cappadocian theologians who now took the lead amongst the Orthodox – Basil of Caesarea, his brother, Gregory of Nyssa, and Gregory of Nazianzus. They held their views strongly and, at times, pugnaciously, but they were less intransigent than Athanasius and reconciled many congregations that he had offended. They opposed the use of physical force in dealing with heretics. Their attitude to the Emperor was Eusebian. He was the Viceroy of God; but it was the duty of the priesthood to guide him into the true spiritual path. He needed its help to become the Christian philosopher-king. Theodosius greatly respected them and listened to them.[10]

Theodosius was less fortunate in his relations with the leading Western saint of the time, Ambrose of Milan. Ambrose had been full of deference towards the Emperor Gratian, of whom he approved. But when Gratian's successor in the West, Valentinian II, tried to hand over a basilica to the Arians, Ambrose told him: 'Do not think that you have any imperial right over things that are divine.'[11] When after the death of Valentinian II Theodosius came to Italy to take over the whole Empire, and there ordered the Bishop of Callinicum to rebuild a synagogue which the bishop had encouraged his flock to loot, Ambrose publicly rebuked the Emperor in a sermon for meddling in holy affairs.[12] Ambrose was in a stronger ethical position when he refused communion to

Theodosius for having ordered his troops to massacre the riotous populace of Thessalonica. Theodosius acknowledged his crime. The story was exaggerated by later historians in the West; but it should be remembered that the Western Church did not fully accept the Eusebian theory: as the future was to show.[13]

It was probably due to Ambrose's influence that Theodosius took action to suppress paganism. A series of decrees issued towards the end of his reign first forbade pagan sacrifices. Next, the chief pagan temples were closed. He intended to secularize them and was angry when Christian fanaticism resulted in their destruction. After the revolt of the pagan Arbogastes in 393 he introduced sterner measures. By the end of the century all the pagan oracles and festivals had been abolished, and pagans could only carry on their worship in private.[14]

In the meantime there had been a significant change in ecclesiastical organization. One of Constantine's finest acts of statemanship had been to found a new capital for the Empire on the site of the city of Byzantium. New Rome, or Constantinople, was ideally placed for the purpose. It was easy of access but easily defensible, with an admirable harbour and a fertile hinterland. The Emperors with their multifarious duties did not often reside there until the end of the century; but the civil service was increasingly concentrated there, especially under Theodosius, and the population of the city grew rapidly. The bishop of Byzantium had been a suffragan of the Metropolitan of Heraclea. But obviously the bishop of a huge capital city should have a higher position. Soon the Bishop of Constantinople began to rank alongside of the bishops of Old Rome, of Alexandria and of Antioch. At the Council of Constantinople, owing to the Emperor's liking for tidiness, these great sees were arranged in order, Constantinople being placed after Rome, with Alexandria and Antioch following. The relevant canon was not accepted by Rome and was angrily contested by Alexandria; but the new order soon came to be recognized.[15] In the course of the next century these great hierarchs were given the title of Patriarch, though the bishop of Rome preferred to call himself Pope and the bishop of Alexandria called himself Patriarch and Pope; and the see of Jerusalem was added to the Patriarchates, because of its holiness rather than because of its material importance.[16] Theodosius emphasized the new position of Constantinople when in July 381 he issued an edict ruling that the true faith was guaranteed by communion with Constantinople and Antioch and 'the chief sees of the East', which are listed but which seem to have been chosen because of the personal eminence of their bishops. Certain historic sees, such as Ephesus and Nicomedia, are omitted, no doubt to underline their inferiority to Constantinople.[17]

Theodosius I died at Milan in January 395, be-

queathing the eastern half of the Empire to his elder
son, Arcadius, who was already reigning as viceroy
in Constantinople, and the western half to his younger
son, Honorius. The Empire was still considered to
be one, and Imperial orders and decrees were issued
in the name of both Emperors, whichever inaugurated
them. The miserable reign of Honorius does not
directly concern us. Arcadius's reign was of high
importance in Byzantine constitutional history. He
was the first Emperor to reside entirely in Constantinople. Previous Emperors had been continually on the
move. Arcadius seldom stirred outside of the city
walls, and seldom, indeed, showed himself outside
of the Great Palace. With the Court permanently
fixed in one spot, the Court ceremonies which the
Emperors had long encouraged could now be developed and systematized. There were still to be
many warrior Emperors who led their armies on
campaigns; but in Constantinople the Emperor began
to be a remote figure who only appeared in public
on ritual occasions, his courtiers in attendance, surrounded by the pomp and the mystery that befitted
the Viceroy of God. At the same time the influence
of the civil service grew, as it was in continual touch
with the Emperor; and, for the same reason, so did
the influence of the Empress.[18] It is significant that
Arcadius's wife Eudoxia is the first Empress of whose
coronation there is any record. Henceforward the
Augusta had her share in the ceremonial mystique.[19]

All the same, behind the trappings the Imperial pair were but mortal beings, as Arcadius and Eudoxia were to be reminded. If Theodosius I had hoped that by raising the Bishop of Constantinople to the primacy of the Eastern Church he would have the chief of the Eastern hierarchy living at his Palace gates at his beck and call, he was overly optimistic. In 398 Arcadius secured the appointment to the see of Constantinople of a distinguished and eloquent preacher, John, surnamed Chrysostom, the 'golden-mouthed'. Chrysostom was an impulsive and inconsistent man. No one was readier than he to regard the earthly Empire as the reflexion of the Heavenly Realm, and he thoroughly approved of the ceremonial etiquette that surrounded the Emperor. But he was an ascetic, and he was horrified by the contrast between the vast wealth and selfish extravagance of the upper classes in the capital and the terrible poverty in the slums. He believed that women should enjoy the same rights as their husbands over property and as regards conjugal infidelity, but at the same time he considered that women had a frivolous and unhealthy influence over men. It was not long before he quarrelled with the pious but splendour-loving Empress. He first accused her of annexing property that rightfully belonged to a poor widow. There was a reconciliation. But then he took offence because she sought the blessing of a dying saint, Epiphanius of Cyprus, whom he suspected of having intrigued against him.

34

He therefore preached in the church of Saint Sophia a violent sermon against women, with references to Jezebel, glaring at the Empress while he spoke. She was furious. With the help of Theophilus, Bishop of Alexandria, who was jealous of his see and his influence, she persuaded Arcadius to summon a Council to depose him. Chrysostom was much loved in the city, and popular riots broke out, followed by an earthquake. The superstitious Empress had him recalled and tried to placate him. On his return Chrysostom preached a fulsome eulogy of the Empress. All might have been well had not the city authorities decided to erect a silver image of Eudoxia on a porphyry column just outside the doors of Saint Sophia; the inaugural ceremonies, which were in the old pagan tradition, with music and dancing, disturbed a service in the church. This enraged Chrysostom, who next Sunday preached a sermon beginning with the words: 'Herodias is raging again. Again she is dancing. Again she demands the head of John on a charger.' After that the Imperial couple and the Bishop were not on speaking terms; and after six months, in June 404, Arcadius, who had hesitated to punish so popular a prelate, declared Chrysostom deposed, and exiled him. On the night of his departure a fire broke out which destroyed not only Saint Sophia but the Senate House next door also. Chrysostom and his friends were accused of arson. He died in exile in 407.[20]

Chrysostom was not a theologian but a moralist. He had attacked the Court on moral grounds, and in so doing he had the support of popular opinion. It is true that his victim was not the Emperor but the Empress, who did not hold so sacred a position. But his attack on the Empress was a clear if indirect attack on the Emperor; and it established the role of the Patriarch of Constantinople as keeper of the Empire's conscience. On matters of morals the Emperor must listen to the priesthood.[21]

Soon, however, a new theological issue threatened Christian unity. The fifth century in the East was dominated by disputes on the exact nature of Christ; and the disputes were embittered by the rivalries of the great episcopal sees. The Church of Alexandria, especially after its rejection of Arius, tended to emphasize the divinity of Christ; the Church of Antioch tended to emphasize His humanity. In 428 Theodosius II, the son of Arcadius, appointed to the see of Constantinople an Antiochene preacher, Nestorius: who soon raised a storm by suggesting that the Virgin Mary should not be called the mother of God. This outraged Cyril, Bishop of Alexandria, who was not displeased at the opportunity of pronouncing his brother of Constantinople to be heretical. The quarrel, which involved the humanity of Christ, soon spread through all the Eastern Churches. It is significant that both Nestorius and Cyril looked to the Emperor for help, not for him to pronounce on doctrine but for him to summon a Council where the true doctrine should be pronounced. 'Give me the earth purged of heretics', wrote Nestorius to the Emperor, 'and I will give you heaven as a reward.'[22] Cyril, who was more unscrupulous but more tactful, wrote to inform 'the Image of God on earth' of the existence of heresy about the Mother of God.[23] Theodosius did not possess the strength of character of his grandfather and namesake. He dithered. He rather liked Nestorius, largely because his eldest sister, Pulcheria, who had bullied him for years, disliked the bishop; and he was annoyed with Cyril, who had appealed behind his back to the Bishop of Rome and had encouraged him to hold a Council in Rome which declared Nestorius desposed. Theodosius could not accept that; so, in nominal association with the Western Emperor, Valentinian III, he summoned a Council, known as the Third Oecumenical Council, to meet at Ephesus in 431. He did not attend it himself; and his representative, Count Candidian, was quite unable to control the proceedings. Cyril of Alexandria arrived first, with nearly two hundred bishops in his train. John, Bishop of Antioch, and his party were delayed; and Nestorius and his party refused to take part in debates till they should be there. Despite the protests of Candidian, Cyril insisted on opening the Council with only his own supporters present. Nestorius was declared to be deposed. When John of Antioch arrived, he and

Nestorius's party held a rival Council in a neighbouring church, over which Candidian presided. It
declared Cyril to be deposed. Candidian then tried
to bring the two Councils together, but in vain. When
Theodosius was informed, he temporized. He recognized both Councils and declared both Nestorius
and Cyril desposed. Nestorius retired with dignity
to a monastery, but was then sent into exile. Cyril,
whose agents had bought him support amongst the
monks of Constantinople, returned defiantly to
his see, with the full support of Rome and the
West.[24]

Theodosius showed equal ineptitude when the
controversy was renewed a few years later. Cyril
died in 444. Soon afterwards an aged abbot in
Constantinople, Eutyches, who had been an agent of
Cyril's, preached a doctrine that Christ had only one
nature, which was divine. It was the logical development of Cyril's view, but it seemed heretical to
Flavian, Bishop of Constantinople. A synod under
his direction condemned it. Thereupon Dioscurus of
Alexandria, Cyril's successor, came out in support of
it. Both sides tried to gain the sympathy of Rome:
whose bishop, Leo I (the Great), pronounced against
Eutyches. There was, Leo thought, no need for a
Council, though he would not object to one held in
the West; and he wrote a statement, a *tomus*, which
gave what he held to be the correct doctrine. That
should settle the matter. The Emperor thought other-

wise. There must be a Council and it must be held
in the East. But he had learnt nothing from previous
experience. He allowed it to be held at Ephesus
again, and he allowed the Alexandrian bishop to
control it. Dioscurus came with a bodyguard of
oriental monks who were ready to manhandle opponents; and the Imperial Commissioners did nothing
to restrain them. The Roman delegates were not
allowed to be present. Flavian was deposed. Eutyches
was pronounced to be Orthodox; and one of his
supporters, Anatolius, was raised to the see of Constantinople. The Emperor weakly concurred. This
'Robber Council', as Leo called it, damaged the
prestige of both the see of Constantinople and the
Emperor himself.[25]

Theodosius II died in 450, a sadly smudged Image
of God. It might have seemed that Imperial authority
over the Church was lost for ever. He had no son;
and his sister, Pulcheria, whom he had crowned
Augusta many years before, now used her position
to nominate his successor, an elderly general, Marcian,
whom she married. This was the first instance of
what later became the constitutional practice: that
in default of an Emperor the senior Empress had
the authority to transmit the Imperial power.[26]
Pulcheria had always disapproved of her brother's
feebleness. She and her husband were in the tradition
of Constantine and Theodosius I. Ignoring Leo the
Great's protests, they summoned a Council to meet

in the East, at Nicaea; but on second thoughts they moved it to Chalcedon, where they could more easily supervise it. Pope Leo sulkily agreed to be represented; to placate him his delegate was given the first place at the Council and the *tomus* of Leo was used as the basis for the discussion. But the *tomus*, in its simple Latin, missed the points which the subtle Greeks were discussing. So some formulae of Cyril of Alexandria were added. Christ was pronounced to have two natures, without confusion or change but without division or separation, each nature ($\phi\acute{v}\sigma\iota s$) concurring into one person ($\acute{v}\pi\acute{o}\sigma\tau\alpha\sigma\iota s$). It was a compromise. The West could accept it, even though the Pope was annoyed that the *tomus* had not been accepted without discussion. The followers of Cyril could not object to it, while Nestorius in his exile pronounced it to be admissible. Other canons of the Council were less generally welcomed. Dioscurus of Alexandria was deposed, his former friends such as Anatolius of Constantinople not daring to vote in his favour. The see of Constantinople was pronounced to have privileges equal to those of the see of Rome, a canon which, though Rome's precedence was admitted, the Roman delegates refused to ratify. The Emperor was careful to stress that the decisions were the bishops', not his own. But he and the Empress had attended some of the sessions, Pulcheria being the first woman to be present at a Council; and their officials had firmly guided the voting. The compromise formula, like

Constantine's at Nicaea, owed its origin to the Emperor, or, more probably, to the Empress.[27]

But the formula, like Constantine's, did not bring peace. The Armenian bishops arrived late for the Council and refused to be bound by its findings, as did many bishops in Egypt and Syria who had refused to attend it at all. Military force was needed to place the successor of Dioscurus, Proterius, on the Alexandrian throne. No sooner was Marcian dead than the Alexandrians murdered Proterius and replaced him by certain Timothy Aelurus, who was an Eutychian, or a Monophysite, as the heretics were now called. Juvenal of Jerusalem, who had signed the decrees of Chalcedon, had to flee for his life when he tried to return to his city, whose leading citizen, Theodosius II's widow Eudocia, favoured the Monophysites until she was cured of her errors by a stern message sent to her by Saint Symeon the Stylite from his pillar near Aleppo.[28] While the Monophysites still hoped to bring the Emperor round to their view, the extreme followers of Nestorius, disregarding their leader's moderation, seceded entirely from the Church and formed their own body, moving their headquarters to the dominions of the Persian King, out of the Emperor's reach. They no longer saw themselves as citizens of the Holy Empire.[29]

The theological problem had still to be solved. But henceforward the Emperor retained the initiative. Marcian's successor, Leo I, tried to hold a sort of referendum. He wrote round to all the chief Churches to collect their views. They all wrote back to praise the Emperor for his pious regard for the Church, comparing him to King David, to Saint Paul and even to Saint Peter. Even the Pope referred to him as a priest. But the answers were theologically un-helpful.[30] His ultimate successor, Zeno, was more direct. He had been for a year ousted by an usurper, Basiliscus, who offended both Constantinople and Rome by patronizing the Monophysites. When Zeno recovered the throne Pope Simplicius wrote to con-gratulate him. 'We rejoice to see in you the spirit of a most faithful priest and prince', he said.[31] But Zeno wished to conciliate the Monophysites, who now dominated Egypt and Syria. Basiliscus had issued an encyclical in his own name which denounced the Council of Chalcedon and the *tomus* of Pope Leo. Quite apart from the heretical nature of the encyclical, Church opinion was shocked by an Emperor pro-nouncing on his own about theology, without refer-ence to a Council.[32] Zeno, however, now followed suit. In 481 he issued, in the form of a letter to the Church of Egypt, a document known as the *henoticon*, the 'unifier', which declared the Creeds of Nicaea and Constantinople to be sufficient and anathematized anyone who had taught divergent doctrines 'at Chalcedon or elsewhere'. Thus, though the findings of Chalcedon were not specifically condemned, it was no longer necessary to accept them. The Monophysites with only a few exceptions were satisfied; but public opinion in Constantinople was disquieted, and Rome was furious. Once again an Emperor was pronouncing upon doctrine, and in so doing implicitly rejecting the *tomus* of Pope Leo. Pope Felix III sternly told Zeno to submit to priests on matters of faith. But he tactfully, and probably rightly, regarded the Bishop – or Patriarch, as he was now called – of Constantinople, Acacius, as having inspired the *henoticon*; and it was Acacius whom he excommunicated. The *henoticon* succeeded in maintaining a precarious religious peace in the East for thirty years, but at the cost of schism with Rome. Meanwhile opinion in the West hardened against the divine position of the Emperor.[33]

When Zeno died without surviving children in 491, his widow, the Empress Ariadne, was required to choose his successor. She nominated a distinguished Senator, Anastasius, who was an amateur theologian. Since Leo I's accession, when there had been no Emperor or Empress living to perform the coronation ceremony, the duty of crowning the Emperor had been given to the Patriarch of Constantinople.[34] The Patriarch Euphemius, who was suspicious of Anastasius, refused to crown him unless he signed a declaration of faith which the Patriarch could accept as Orthodox. Anastasius readily signed the document; and no one seems to have remarked that it made a dangerous precedent. In any case, Anastasius ignored its terms and showed favour to the Monophysites, maintaining the *henoticon* as the official basis for doctrine. This was not liked in Constantinople, where there were riots when on two occasions he deposed an Orthodox Patriarch – Euphemius and Macedonius – and even rebellion. But Anastasius managed to remain on the throne for twenty-seven years and died comfortably of old age.[35]

His policy inevitably annoyed Rome. The line of Western Emperors had ended either with the deposition of the child Romulus Augustulus in 476, as was generally thought in the West, or, as Byzantine jurists thought, with the death of Julius Nepos in 480. Thenceforward Zeno and, after him, Anastasius were legally rulers of the undivided Empire. In fact they had no more authority in the West than the German chieftains who ruled there chose to give them.[36] The Popes, much as they disliked the Arian Gothic masters of Italy, disliked a Monophysite Emperor almost more strongly. After the excommunication of the Patriarch Acacius they refused to recognize any of his successors, even those who were correctly Orthodox and wished to resume relations. When Gelasius I succeeded to the Papacy in 492 he neglected the customary courtesy of informing the Emperor and asking for his confirmation. Anastasius wrote to protest; Gelasius replied in a letter which was to become a fundamental statement of future Papal theory. In it he declared that the world was governed by two things, the authority of the pontiffs and the power of the Emperor, and of these the priestly authority was the greater, for priests are responsible before God even for princes. Priests should obey the Emperor's laws in worldly matters; but the Emperor must obey those who administer the sacred Mysteries. That is to say, the Emperor must not interfere in theology or even in the government of the Church, though he must summon Church Councils when required to do so by the hierarchy.[37]

Anastasius was not pleased. He wrote to the Pope telling him to imitate the humility of Christ, and added: 'We can stand insult, but we cannot take orders.' When writing a little later to the Roman Senate he deliberately gave himself the title of *Pontifex Inclytus*. The *imperium* was not to be deprived of its priestly character.[38]

The next Emperor, the Illyrian peasant Justin, urged by his nephew and heir, Justinian, ended the schism with Rome by abandoning the *henotikon* and by admitting the special primacy of Rome in the Church.[39] Justinian wished to re-establish Imperial authority in the West and saw that he therefore needed the goodwill of Rome. But he did not subscribe to the Gelasian doctrine. Indeed, his reign (527–65) is usually, and rightly, regarded as marking the zenith of Imperial dominance over the Church, a dominance that is all the more remarkable as Justinian could never make up his own mind on theological questions. He had no doubts about the role of the Emperor. Phrases like: 'By the will of God we govern an Empire that has come to us from His Divine Majesty', or 'God alone, and the Emperor who follows God, can rule the world with justice', flowed readily from his pen. The Emperor must copy God in charity, by 'benevolence, by which alone the imitation of God is effected'. His authority extends over the priesthood. Justinian drew a distinction between the *sacerdotium* and the *imperium* and rated the former as the higher, stating that their harmony is essential to the welfare of the world. But it is for the Emperor to secure and supervise that harmony. The *imperium* will always, he says, support the decision and the authority of the priests; but his words, 'God's true dogmas and the priests' dignity are therefore our first concern', show where he believed the ultimate authority to lie. His separation of the *imperium* and the *sacerdotium* did not keep him from legislating on religious matters; and his treatment of the hierarchy was high-handed, to say the least.[40]

His high-handedness was all the more arbitrary because of his indecision. He soon realized that if he conciliated Rome he would offend the Monophysites who formed the bulk of his subjects in Egypt and Syria; and his wife, Theodora, who not only had a strong influence over him but was also quite ready to conduct a separate policy of her own, had Monophysite sympathies. His first attempt at compromise was to pronounce that the true faith lay in the Theo-paschite formula, put forward by four Scythian monks who maintained that 'one of the Trinity suffered in the flesh'.[41] But the Monophysites considered this a meaningless concession; and though Pope John II in 533 gave a grudging approval to the doctrine, it was fiercely contested by the most powerful monastic community in Constantinople, the Sleepless monks of Sosthenion, so-called because their services lasted unceasingly day and night.[42] Then in 535 Justinian allowed Theodora to nominate a Patriarch of Constantinople, Anthimus, who at once associated himself with the Monophysite Patriarchs of Alexandria and Jerusalem. The anti-Monophysite Patriarch of Antioch reported this to Pope Agapetus, who hastened to Constantinople and persuaded Justinian to depose and exile Anthimus and his Alexandrian colleague. They disappeared; and it was not till Theodora's death in 548 that Justinian discovered that they had been living all the intervening years in comfort in Theodora's apartments in the Palace.[43] There followed a persecution of the Monophysites which Theodora determined to end. Agapetus had died in 536; and as his successor, Silverius, refused to re-instate Anthimus, she arranged with the Imperial commander in Italy, Belisarius, to have Silverius arrested and exiled, and replaced by Vigilius, who had been Papal nuncio in Constantinople and had given the Empress to understand that he was less intransigent. But

Vigilius, once he had secured the Papacy, proved equally obdurate. A tactful nuncio at the Imperial Court, Pelagius, managed to placate the Empress, but she never forgave Vigilius for having deceived her.[44]

Meanwhile Justinian had been persuaded that if the works of three divines, Theodore of Mopsuestia, Theodoret and Ibas, which had opposed Cyril of Alexandria's views but which had been tacitly endorsed at Chalcedon, were anathematized, the Monophysites would be mollified. The four Patriarchs were consulted and grudgingly concurred with the anathema, so long as their brother of Rome agreed. Vigilius made it clear that he would not agree. So at the end of 545 he was ruthlessly kidnapped and carried to Constantinople, where his vacillations were only equalled by the physical indignities that he suffered. In 546 Justinian issued an edict condemning the Three Chapters, as the works in question were called. Vigilius at last gave his consent to the edict but demanded that it should be confirmed by an Oecumenical Council, which he then refused to attend. The Fifth Oecumenical Council met in Constantinople in 553 and duly anathematized the Three Chapters and also the Pope: who saved himself by then concurring with the condemnation. He was allowed to return homeward but died on the journey. His successor, the tactful Pelagius, endorsed the decisions of the Council. But many bishops and Churches in the West ignored the Council and its findings. It has never ranked as an Oecumenical Council there.[45]

Justinian's imperious policy was to no avail. The Monophysites had been discouraged by the death of Theodora in 548 and remained unmollified. During the last years of the reign the Syrian Monophysites were organized by Jacob Baradaeus, heretic Bishop of Edessa, into a separate Church, secret and persecuted at first, but soon to capture the allegiance of the majority of the Syrians. It is still called the Jacobite Church after him. In Egypt, too, the Monophysites were moving towards the creation of their own separated Coptic Church.[46]

In his old age Justinian tried once again to have a compromise doctrine accepted when he gave his approval to Aphthartodocetism, a dogma that had been proposed by Julian of Halicarnassus, which declared that Christ's body was incorruptible from the moment that it was entered by the *logos*. The Patriarch Eutychius who denounced it was sent into exile. The other Patriarchs also protested, but were saved by the Emperor's death, in November 565.[47]

Justinian had genuinely thought it his duty to bring unity to the Church; but his efforts had failed. No one in the East, however annoyed he might be that the Emperor did not show him sympathy, questioned the Imperial right to make pronouncements, so long as they were later endorsed by a Council. Even in the West his autocratic treatment of the Popes caused curiously little resentment, perhaps because the Popes of the time were of a poor calibre, and perhaps, still more, because of the presence of an Imperial army in Italy. When the physical force of the Empire was withdrawn, the West reverted to the Gelasian doctrine, with its division of powers. The idea of the Holy Empire could not exist if there were no effective Imperial authority. Saint Augustine had already taught the West that the City of God had other foundations. In the East it was not Justinian's methods that caused bitterness but their ineffectuality. He had given so much of his attention to the unity of Christendom; and already before he had died separated Churches had arisen to which he was no longer the Viceroy of God.[48]

3

THE BATTLE OVER IMAGES:
THE CHALLENGE OF POPULAR
BELIEF

Justinian's successors inherited his problems and his methods. His nephew, Justin II, though Orthodox himself, still hoped to win back the Monophysites. Early in his reign he summoned a Council to meet at Callinicum, on the Syrian border; but its first session ended in a riot. In 571 he issued a *Programma*, sometimes called the *Second Henoticum*, an elaborately worded document which was basically Orthodox but made no mention of Chalcedon. A few moderate Monophysites subscribed to it; but it failed to satisfy general Monophysite opinion. The Emperor was exasperated, and next year, encouraged by a fanatical Patriarch, John of Sirimis, he annulled the orders of Monophysite priests and closed monasteries that were suspected of Monophysite sympathies, while prominent men and women who were attached to the heresy were imprisoned unless they recanted.[1] This merely encouraged separatist tendencies amongst the heretics.

Justin went mad in 574. The Empress Sophia then selected a promising young soldier, Tiberius, to be

Caesar and regent. He succeeded to the Empire on Justin's death in 578. He was an efficient military reformer whose attention was devoted to a war against the Persians and to seeking popularity by reducing taxation at a moment when the Treasury was almost empty. Apart from a desultory persecution of the Monophysites, he showed very little interest in religion.[2]

His son-in-law Maurice, who succeeded him in 582, was an able general whose eyes were fixed on the East, and was therefore eager to recapture the goodwill of the Monophysites. He showed them tolerance; and, to simplify future religious policy, he planned to give to the Patriarch of Constantinople an authority over the Eastern Patriarchs similar to that which the Bishop of Rome enjoyed over the whole Western Church. He therefore encouraged the Patriarch, John the Faster, officially to assume the title of 'Oecumenical', a title which the Patriarch of Constantinople bears to this day. In Byzantine Greek the word 'Oecumene' had come to mean the Empire itself, not, as it literally meant, the whole inhabited world; and it might seem suitable that the bishop of the capital city of the Empire should have the title.[3] The results were not what Maurice had intended. The Eastern Patriarchs, whether their sympathies were Chalcedonian or Monophysite, had no wish to cede their autonomy to a see that they regarded as parvenu nor to accept meekly theological

rulings imposed on them by Constantinople. The
Pope, Gregory the Great, was outraged at John the
Faster's assuming a title which, in his opinion, could
only be applied rightly to himself. He sent a furious
protest to the Emperor. He did not, however, follow
the Gelasian doctrine. On the contrary, the Emperor
was told that it was his duty to bring peace to the
Church. No one, said Gregory, can govern the state
unless he knows how to deal with divine matters.
Maurice must order the Patriarch to cease from
troubling the established pattern of the Church.
Gregory wrote also to the Empress Constantina,
informing her that John the Faster's presumption
was a sure sign that Antichrist was at hand. Maurice
was unmoved, and further annoyed Gregory by
issuing a law forbidding civil servants from entering
a monastery until the time had come for their retirement. To Gregory, who had been a civil servant and
had abandoned his office to become a monk, this
seemed a personal insult. When in 602 Maurice was
dethroned by the usurper Phocas and brutally
murdered along with his young children, Gregory
sent delighted congratulations to the new Emperor,
saying that angelic choirs would be singing a *gloria*
in heaven at the news; and he continued to shower
praise on Phocas throughout what was the most
savage reign of terror in all Byzantine history.[4]

By his folly Phocas provoked a fresh outbreak of
war with Persia; and his incompetence enabled the

Persians to penetrate into the heart of the Empire. They occupied most of Syria, while one raiding force made its way as far as the shores of the Bosphorus, devastating Asia Minor as it came. At this moment Phocas decided not only to revive the persecution of the Monophysites but also to force all the Jewish communities in Syria to adopt Christianity. This, not unnaturally, caused riots in both Jewish and heretic circles. The Persians were welcomed as deliverers. Meanwhile Slavs were pouring across the Danube into the Balkans; and behind them was the military power of the Avars.[5]

The Empire was saved by Heraclius, a young general of Armenian descent, the son of the governor of Africa. He sailed to Constantinople and dethroned Phocas in 610. Eighteen years were to pass before the Persians were crushed and the Avars driven back. During those years the Persians were in possession not only of Syria and Palestine but also of Egypt. The local inhabitants, nearly all Monophysites, did nothing to oppose them: though there was a shock throughout Christendom when in 615 the invaders took the holiest of Christian relics, the True Cross which the Empress Helena had found, from its shrine in Jerusalem. This humiliation was so deeply felt in Constantinople that the Patriarch Sergius of his own accord offered a loan from the Church to the State. Church revenues were handed over to the Emperor. Church vessels were melted down that he might have the metal in them. The war had become a Holy War. The Treasury had been empty after the extravagance of Phocas and the loss of revenues from Egypt and Syria. It was the Church that enabled Heraclius to pay for his campaigns. He himself had been in such despair that he had planned to move the capital to Carthage, a city that could at least be victualled; for Constantinople depended on corn from Egypt and was near to starvation. His plan appalled the Constantinopolitans, who, led by Sergius, begged him not to desert them and agreed to give up the dole of free bread, which had been the right of every citizen in the capital since Roman days and which the government could no longer afford.[6]

The Persians were at last utterly defeated; and in 629 Heraclius solemnly restored the Holy Cross to its shrine in Jerusalem. But the problem of the Monophysites remained unsolved. Already in the middle of the war Heraclius had put forward a dogma suggested to him by the Patriarch; that Christ had two natures but one Energy, or operation. Sergius believed this to be the logical outcome of the Chalcedonian doctrine, but both he and the Emperor thought that it would be acceptable to the Monophysites. Heraclius in particular hoped that it would satisfy his Armenian compatriots. It won support at first. The Monophysite Patriarchs of Alexandria and Antioch, Athanasius and Cyrus, were willing to subscribe to it. But there were many Chalcedonians who suspected it as a gesture to please the heretics. They found a leader in a Palestinian monk, Sophronius, who became Patriarch of Jerusalem in 634. To silence his Chalcedonian critics Sergius appealed to the Pope, Honorius I, who did not quite understand the point at issue but gave Sergius his general support.[7]

Soon, however, it was clear that Orthodox opinion disliked the doctrine of One Energy, while the Mono-physites were less and less interested in a compromise. Sergius therefore drew up a declaration of faith, known as the *Ecthesis*, which forbade discussion on the Energies but declared that Christ had only one Will, a phrase that Pope Honorius had used in his reply to Sergius. Sergius wished the *Ecthesis* to be backed by Imperial authority; but Heraclius was not happy about it and only put his name to it late in 638, out of deference to Sergius, for whom he felt friendship and gratitude. But Monotheletism, the doctrine of One Will, was no more to the liking of the Orthodox than the doctrine of One Energy.[8] And in the meantime the Monophysite problem had been for practical purposes solved in a more drastic and untheological manner.

Hardly had the Persian war ended before nomads from the Arabian desert, inspired by the faith of the Prophet Mohammed, burst into the cultivated lands of Syria. The first clash had occurred in 622, during the Persian war; but it was in 634, two years after the Prophet's death, that the deliberate invasion began. The invaders won a decisive battle by the river Yarmuk that autumn. Damascus fell to them early next year. Jerusalem, from which the Emperor had prudently rescued all the major Christian relics, fell after a siege of two years in 637, and Antioch in 638. Late in 639 the Arabs entered Egypt. When Heraclius died early in 641, all that rich province was lost to the Empire except for Alexandria; and it fell a few months later.[9]

The Monophysites of Syria and Egypt had passively accepted Persian dominion. But the Persians were alien to them in race and in religion. The Arabs were their kinsfolk. Nearly all of them were the descendants of earlier invaders from the desert; and in recent centuries there had been a constant infiltration from over the Arabian frontier and across the Red Sea. Islam, the faith preached by Mohammed, seemed to many of them to be nearer to their own than was Chalcedonian Orthodoxy, the faith of the Greeks and the Romans. They welcomed their new conquerors, who showed them tolerance and who taxed them far less heavily than did the Emperor. Increasing numbers of them became willing converts to the new religion. It was only when they invaded Asia Minor that the Arabs met with resistance from the local population, which was of a different stock and more loyal to Orthodoxy. For centuries to come the frontier between Christendom and Islam ran along the Taurus and Antitaurus mountains that separate the Anatolian highlands from the Syrian plains.[10]

The loss of Syria and Egypt left the Patriarch of Constantinople as the only Patriarch in the East still to live under a Christian government. The Patriarchs of Alexandria, Antioch and Jerusalem inevitably became shadowy and inferior figures who could no longer be used to counterbalance their Constantinopolitan brother. The Emperor now had only one Patriarch within his dominions; and the position of the Patriarch was thereby made more formidable. The religious opposition in Byzantium could now only appeal to the Pope, the Patriarch of the West, for support against the ecclesiastical establishment; and Roman interference was never popular in Constantinople.[11]

It should, however, be remembered that there were still Orthodox communities in the provinces conquered by the Arabs, especially in Palestine: and in that Eastern world where religious affiliation took the place of nationality, these Orthodox, though they might have to obey the laws of the Muslim Caliph in whose lands they lived, still regarded the Orthodox Emperor as their sovereign lord; and this was accepted by the Caliph.[12] The Eastern Patriarchs were seldom prevented from visiting Constantinople, where they were treated with the respect that the high traditions of their sees demanded; and no Council could rank as being Oecumenical unless they or their representatives were present.[13]

Heraclius's grandson, Constans II, who triumphed over his rivals within the family in 642, maintained the doctrine of Monotheletism, even though the loss of the Monophysite provinces had removed its political purpose. When the new Pope, Theodore I, a Greek by birth, protested, Constans issued an edict forbidding further discussion of the Wills of Christ. But the most eminent theologian of the time, the monk Maximus, surnamed the Confessor, refused to be silenced. He strongly disapproved of Monotheletism, and he won the support of Theodore's successor, Martin I, who had already offended the Emperor by neglecting to obtain Imperial confirmation for his appointment. Constans, who wished to compensate for the Empire's losses in the East by re-establishing its authority in Italy, sent troops to Rome, who kidnapped the Pope and sent him to Constantinople. He was roughly treated there, accused of sedition and rebellion and sentenced to death. But the Patriarch Paul of Constantinople, who, though he shared Constans's theological views, was shocked by such brutality towards a hierarch, interceded for him. He was reprieved, but exiled to Cherson in the Crimea, where he died in 658. Constans then prosecuted Maximus the Confessor, an action that upset the Constantinopolitans far more than did the ill treatment of the Pope. It was largely due to his unpopularity in the city that Constans left it in 662 to go to Italy. He first intended to make Old Rome his capital; but, after visiting it in 663, he decided to set up his government at Syracuse, in Sicily: where in 668 he was murdered in his bath by a chamberlain armed with a soap-dish.[14]

His son and successor, Constantine IV, surnamed the Bearded, returned to Constantinople and came to see that there was no longer any possible political value in Monotheletism. In 678 he wrote to the Pope, tactfully addressing him as 'Oecumenical Pope', asking for his co-operation in a General Council, to be held in Constantinople. Pope Agatho gave his approval, and, after himself holding a preliminary Council of the Western Churches, sent three delegates to represent him at what came to be known as the Sixth Oecumenical Council. It sat in the Imperial Palace from November 680 to September 681. The Emperor presided at most of its meetings, with the Patriarchs of Constantinople and Antioch and representatives from Alexandria seated on his right, and the Roman representatives and representatives from Jerusalem on his left. There were eighteen sessions. It was only at the eighth that George of Constantinople agreed to declare himself against Monotheletism; at the ninth Macarius of Antioch refused to abandon the doctrine, together with Stephen, Bishop of Corinth. Both were promptly deposed, the Emperor elevating a certain Theophanes to Antioch. Finally all past and present adherents of the doctrine were condemned, and the names of three Patriarchs of Constantinople and of Pope Honorius himself were removed from the commemorative diptychs of the Patriarchate. The supreme role of the Emperor was fully admitted. After the eighth session the whole assembly rose and chanted: 'Long live the Preserver of the Orthodox Faith, the new Constantine the Great...We are all the slaves of the Emperor.'[15]

Peace was restored to the Church. But under Constantine IV's brilliant, wayward son, Justinian II, fresh trouble arose. In 692 the Emperor summoned a Council to meet in the same domed hall of the Palace, in order to complete the work of the Fifth and Sixth Oecumenical Councils by regularizing Church practices. It is known as the Quinisext Council or the Council in Trullo. But the Papal delegates had long since gone home; and the Council condemned certain practices followed in the West, notably fasting on Saturdays and the celibacy of the clergy. Pope Sergius I therefore refused to confirm its canons; and Justinian's attempt to send troops to Rome to force him to agree to them was a fiasco. There was schism between Rome and Constantinople till 710, when Pope Constantine I courageously accepted an invitation to visit the Emperor, who was known by then to be dangerously mad. Rather surprisingly, Justinian received him with great deference and told him, it seems, that the canons of the Quinisext Council need not be applied to the West.[16]

The reign of Justinian II ended in anarchy in 711. His successor was an Armenian general, Bardanes Philippicus, an old-fashioned Monothelete who publicly burnt the records of the Sixth Oecumenical Council and tried to replace the leading bishops of the Empire with Monotheletes. By now the heresy had no supporters in Constantinople; and when the news reached Rome Pope Constantine refused to recognize the Emperor. Philippicus was dethroned and blinded in 713 as much for his religious policy as for his refusal to make serious preparations against a great invasion launched by the Arabs with the expressed intention of capturing Constantinople. His successor was a worthy civil servant, Anastasius II, who restored peace to the Church and who collected armaments and provisions for the defence of the Empire. But he failed to win the respect of the army, whose irresponsible leaders picked on an obscure and unwilling tax-collector as their candidate for the throne. Anastasius was allowed to retire to a monastery; and for two years Theodosius the tax-collector headed a well-intentioned and hopelessly incompetent government. In 717 he gladly handed over the Imperial power to a new army candidate, Leo III, surnamed the Isaurian.[17]

It was fortunate for the Empire that circumstances obliged the Arabs to delay their invasion. Leo had been on the throne for five months, spent busily in strengthening the defences of the city, when at the end of August a huge Arab army appeared on the shores of the Bosphorus, opposite Constantinople, to be followed a few days later by a huge Arab fleet sailing up the Sea of Marmora.

Twelve months later a small remnant of the Arab army crept back to Syria; and of the vast armada only five ships returned. The Christian victory had been due to the strong walls of the capital, the courage and skill of its soldiers, sailors and engineers, and to the resourcefulness of its diplomats. But the architect of victory had been unquestionably the Emperor himself.[18] He was a man of remarkable ability, energy and intellect; and he determined to use his victory to reform and re-organize the Empire over which he ruled. He was responsible for the completion of the so-called *theme* system by which the provinces of the Empire were henceforward administered. He introduced a revised law-code, the *Ecloga*, and issued improved editions of the maritime and agricultural codes.[19] But his main ambition was to carry out ecclesiastical and theological reforms. He was devout. The *Ecloga* brings a number of Christian principles to bear on the law, especially as regards marriage, and incidentally gives mothers equal rights with fathers over ther children. He was in no doubt about his duties as Emperor. In the preface to the *Ecloga* he writes: 'Since God has put in our hands the

Imperial authority, according to His good pleasure...
bidding us to feed His faithful flock after the manner
of Peter, head and chief of the Apostles, we believe
that there is nothing higher that we can do than to
govern in justice those who are committed to us by
His care.' In the first article law is defined as 'the
discovery of God'. In the second, the Emperor's
duty is defined as the maintenance of all things laid
down in the Scriptures and the enactments of the
Holy Councils and the laws of Rome. The Patriarch
is given the highest position next to the Emperor.
They two are the chief parts in the body politic,
whose welfare depends on their working in harmony.
It is the Patriarch's business to see to the spiritual
well-being of the Empire. But it is the Emperor alone
who can give to the recommendations of the Patriarch
the force of law. His is the ultimate decision on
religious as well as civil affairs. He is still the Viceroy
of God.[20]

Leo therefore believed himself to be entitled to
enforce religious reforms. He was of Syrian origin,
coming from Germanicea, the modern Marash; and
he shared the stern dislike of the Semites for anything
that might smack of idolatry.[21] The taste for images
and holy relics was now widespread throughout
Christendom. Many of the Early Fathers had opposed
its growth, as it seemed to them to contravene the
Old Testament ban on graven images. Eusebius of
Caesarea had angrily rebuked Constantine's sister

Constantia when she asked him to send her a picture of Christ from Palestine.[22] Saint Epiphanius of Cyprus himself tore down a pictured curtain that he saw in a village church.[23] But other Fathers, reared in a Neoplatonic tradition, were more tolerant of images. Saint Basil declares that the honour paid to an icon passes to the prototype and adds that a picture is, as it were, a sermon, a reminder of God and the saints.[24] Leontius of Neapolis, when arguing against Jewish critics, points out that images of cherubim were permitted in the Old Testament, and that anyhow what we revere is not the material of which the image is made, not the beams of wood that make up a cross, but the cross as symbol of the Cross on which Jesus died for men.[25] Against the argument that God by His nature cannot be depicted, the advocates of images replied that to say so was to deny the central doctrine of Christianity, the incarnation of Christ. As incarnate man He could be portrayed, as could without question His mother and all the saints. The angels, creatures of pure spirit, caused a problem. But the Old Testament told of angels being seen by mortal eyes. They too therefore could be depicted.[26]

These were theologians' arguments. The humbler folk in the Empire, whose ancestors a few generations back had been giving full worship to the statues of the gods and goddesses, willingly gave a similar worship to the statues and pictures of Christ and the saints, crediting them, too, with the power to work miracles.[27] In particular, the citizens of Constantinople held that their city was specially protected by the Mother of God. During the siege of the city in 626, when the Persians and the Avars combined to assault the walls, it was the power of her holy image that drove them back. She was again successfully invoked in 677, to defeat an Arab attack; and even Leo III seems to have permitted, if not actually encouraged, her image to be paraded in the streets during the siege of 717.[28]

The Church had given official approval to images. Indeed, the Quinisext Council had ordered that Christ should no longer be depicted symbolically as a lamb, but as a person, so as to emphasize His human nature.[29] Over the main entrance gate to the Sacred Palace there was a great image of Christ, apparently in bas-relief, which tradition now claimed had been placed there by Constantine the Great.[30] Justinian II had carved a head of Christ on his coins, though his immediate successors had not followed his example.[31] Images and relics were to be found in every church building, some to illustrate the Bible story for the illiterate, and others to receive the reverence due to the holy persons that they represented.[32]

Nevertheless there remained a larger number of Christians who disapproved of images. They were to be found mainly in the Eastern provinces of the Empire, where there was a large admixture of Semitic blood. There were some in Constantinople, where in 670 the Western traveller Arculf saw a fanatic destroy an image of the Virgin.[33] In the late seventh century there had been a strong iconoclastic movement in Armenia and the neighbouring districts[34]. In the Muslim world, where pictorial representation had at first been permitted, there was by A.D. 700 a total ban on pictures of the human form and even of animals. In 723 the Caliph Yezid ordered that this ban should be extended to the churches, synagogues and houses of his non-Muslim subjects. The order was only partially carried out and soon abandoned; and it is difficult to believe that it had any great influence on the iconoclasts of Byzantium, who only disapproved of religious images. But it illustrated the dislike of images to be found in many quarters of the Semitic world; and it gave the supporters of images the opportunity of declaring that their opponents were inspired by an infidel religion.[35]

This charge was certainly levelled against Constantine, Bishop of Nacoleia, in Phrygia, who was summoned to Constantinople in 724 or 725 to be reproved by the Patriarch Germanus I for his destruction of images. Bishop Constantine went home pretending to have been convinced by the Patriarch; but it is likely that when in the capital he saw the Emperor, whom he found to share his views.[36] It was rumoured that the Caliph Yezid had been influenced by a Palestinian Jew whom the Greeks nicknamed Sarantapechys, 'forty cubits high'; and Sarantapechys was friendly with a Syrian Christian called Beser, who had been captured by the Arabs and converted to Islam, then had been released and entered the service of the Emperor, who thought highly of him.[37] Whatever encouragement he may have received, by 725 Leo was genuinely and devoutly convinced that images ought not to have any place in Christian worship. He was not without super-stition. A violent eruption in the volcanic island of Santorin that year persuaded him that God was angry with him for delaying action.[38]

He certainly knew that the Patriarch and the higher ecclesiastical authorities did not share his view. But he believed that as Emperor he had the right, the power and the duty to override them. He moved cautiously at first. In 726 he delivered speeches and sermons advocating the removal of images. When these had no effect he ordered, early in 727, the destruction of the icon of Christ over the Palace gate. There was a popular riot; and the official who was carrying out the Emperor's instructions was done to death by furious women. The rioters were severely punished, by scourging, mutilation or exile.[39] This provoked further unrest. Leo could count on the support of the army; for most of his best troops came, as he did, from districts where a certain austerity in religious practice prevailed. But the navy was recruited mainly from the Aegean coasts and islands, where images were eagerly worshipped. In April 727, a naval detachment revolted and sailed on Constantinople. Leo was obliged to destroy the ships by Greek fire, and the ringleaders were put to death.[40] Next, the University was closed because too many professors objected to the Emperor's views.[41] The Patriarch and the hierarchy refused to support the Emperor, who had no greater success when he sought support from Rome. He sent Pope Gregory II a series of treatises on the impropriety of images, and threatened him with deposition if he did not agree with him. Gregory replied with treatises in favour of images, and, while professing loyalty to the Emperor, ignored his religious policy, which had already roused protests in Italy.[42]

Thwarted in his attempts at persuasion, in January 730 the Emperor summoned a *silention*, an assembly of high officials of the Empire, men of his own choosing, to meet in the Palace, in the Triclinium of the Nineteen Couches. It approved an act which he had drawn up, forbidding the cult of images and their presence in churches. The Patriarch Germanus was ordered to subscribe to it, but refused, saying that his faith was that of the Oecumenical Councils. He then cast off his Patriarchal robes and retired to his private house.[43] The Patriarchate was declared to be vacant; but a year elapsed before the Emperor could find a priest willing to assume the dignity and, which was more difficult, a sufficient number of sympathetic bishops to form a synod to elect him. The new Patriarch, Anastasius, then sent round a synodal letter to his fellow-Patriarchs announcing his adherence to the Emperor's doctrine.[44]

The Eastern Patriarchs disapproved but could do nothing. The Pope, Gregory III, who succeeded Gregory II in 731, summoned a Council of the Italian Church which firmly excommunicated destroyers of images. Leo retorted by sending a fleet to enforce his will; but it was dispersed by a storm. He had to content himself with withholding the revenues that the Papacy should receive from Sicily and Calabria; and, more drastically, he transferred the province of Illyricum, which included the western Balkans and Greece, from the Roman Patriarchate to that of Constantinople.[45]

Leo III died in 740. For the last ten years of his reign there had been a steady destruction of icons and holy paintings in Constantinople and to a lesser extent in the provinces. Anyone who tried to hinder the work of destruction was sternly punished, but no one seems to have been put to death.[46] Leo's son and successor, Constantine V, who had already been co-Emperor for twenty years, had every intention of continuing his father's policy. But almost at once he had to face a serious revolt led by his brother-in-law, Artavasdus, who reigned for a year in Constantinople and re-introduced image-worship, aided by the turncoat Patriarch Anastasius. When Constantine recaptured the capital, Anastasius was paraded in the Emperor's triumphal procession, seated on an ass with his face to its tail, being scourged as he rode along. But he remained on the Patriarchal throne, unlikely after his humiliation to cause further trouble. There followed a period of warfare, during which Constantine successfully dealt with the Saracen menace on the Eastern frontier and the Bulgarian one in the Balkans. In Italy the Lombard menace made it advisable for him to keep on good terms with the Pope. Owing to these distractions he took no further steps against image-worship, though he continued publicly to advocate Iconoclasm.[47] It was not till 754 that he felt secure enough to strike against the image-worshippers. He was by now immensely popular with the army. He transferred large colonies of iconoclastic Asiatics into districts in Thrace that had been wholly image-worshipping. For a generation past it had been necessary to have iconoclastic sympathies to win preferment at Court or in the Church; so he could now count on the support of the civil service and the hierarchy.[48] It was believed, at least by his enemies, that his own religious views were extremely heterodox. He was said to have taken a Monophysite attitude towards Christ and a Nestorian attitude towards the Virgin, to have disapproved of the title of 'saint', and even to have sympathized with the neo-Manichaean sect of the Paulicians.[49] He was certainly an able and ingenious theologian, who felt strongly against images; and he decided that the time had come to legitimize Iconoclasm by means of a General Council of the Church.

Leo III had issued his decree against Iconoclasm on his own authority as Emperor, considering himself to be Pontifex, a priest-king, as he told the Pope. He had been more high-handed than even Justinian I; he had used a lay assembly through which to promulgate a religious law, and he had re-arranged ecclesiastical provinces without any reference to a Council. Rome had naturally protested on both counts. In Constantinople, where the transfer of Illyricum had not been unwelcome, the Patriarch Germanus had reflected public opinion when he protested that only a Council could declare the Faith. But the Emperor, with the army behind him and his own personal prestige, was too powerful to be challenged from within his dominions. It was only from outside that protests could be made. The Papal treatises had little effect within the Empire. It was, ironically, from the safety of the Caliph's dominions that Iconoclasm received its sharpest attack. Saint John of Damascus came from a Syrian Christian family and, till his retirement into a Syrian monastery, had been, like his father and his grandfather before him, an official in the Caliph's Treasury. But he regarded himself as a citizen of the Oecumene, always addressing the Emperor as his lord and master and referring to the Caliph merely as the 'Emir'. His three great orations against Iconoclasm were to be the basis of all future ones. He reminded the Emperor that it was for the ordained pastors of the Church to pronounce on doctrine and the ecclesiastical pattern, and he learnedly refuted the accusation of idolatry. But he did not deal with the subtle Christological arguments that Constantine V was to introduce.[50]

Constantine was more fanatical but more correct than his father. He saw that his policy must be endorsed by a Council. In 752 and 753 *silentia* were held throughout the provinces, where his officials explained his doctrines and argued with image-worshippers.[51] In February 754, he opened a Council of the Church at Hieria, near Chalcedon. The Iconoclasts were to call it the Seventh Oecumenical Council; but, as neither the Pope nor any of the Eastern Patriarchs were represented, it could not claim oecumenicity. It sat for six months. The Patriarch Anastasius had died; and, as no new Patriarch had been elected, the president was Theodore, Metropolitan of Ephesus, who had been a disciple of Constantine of Nacoleia. Three hundred and thirty-two bishops were present. Constantine must have made sure that he could count on their support. But, even so, long discussions were needed before an agreed statement on doctrine could be issued. The *Horos*, which was undoubtedly inspired by the Emperor, declared that the holy Emperor had been moved by the Holy Spirit to destroy the new idolatry which the malice of Satan had created. Images of Christ were denounced as being heretical, while it was an insult to the Virgin and the saints to depict them in an earthly form. Anyone who made an icon or worshipped one or placed one in a church or even in a private house was, if a cleric, to be unfrocked and, if a monk or a layman, to be excommunicated; and all would then be punished under the laws of the Empire. But no building was to be entered nor anything destroyed, even by officials, without the authorization of the Emperor and the Patriarch. Having secured this ecclesiastical backing, and having soon afterwards appointed a new and complaisant Patriarch, Constantine II, the Emperor issued an edict that heretics would be treated as rebels against the State.[52]

Constantine seems to have hoped that his subjects would all accept a doctrine backed by a Council of the Church. Official classes naturally supported it, and it was popular in the army and in the Eastern provinces from which most of the soldiers came. But in the European provinces and in Western Anatolia the bulk of the population continued to be devoted to images. Even in the capital, in spite of the presence of the Emperor and his troops and his police, image-worship could not be stamped out. The Emperor had his supporters there, as the lynching of Saint Stephen the Younger was to show. But the opposition had the support of the monasteries. The Emperor was able to control the bishops. He could not exercise the same control over abbots and monks. The monks became the leaders of the people.[53]

The continued opposition exasperated Constantine. In 761 he launched a fierce persecution of image-worshippers, with the monks as the chief victims. Monasteries and nunneries were pulled down and their inhabitants ordered to marry or else be exiled. In 765 a number of recalcitrant monks were forced to parade in the Hippodrome, each escorting a noted prostitute. At least six monks were put to death. Laymen and laywomen who would not conform were imprisoned and tortured or banished. The persecution was most severe in or near Constantinople; but certain provincial governors won the Emperor's approval by their exceptional savagery, in particular Michael Lachanodragon, whose district included Smyrna and Ephesus.[54]

After some six years the persecution was relaxed. The Emperor was distracted by fresh wars against the Bulgarians; and it may be that he was becoming aware that the popular opposition to Iconoclasm was too strong to be overcome by making martyrs of the monks. In this he was probably influenced by a new Patriarch. In 765 the Patriarch Constantine II, who had supported the persecutions, had been found guilty of treason and had been brutally put to death. His successor, Nicetas I, a Slav in origin, advocated a milder policy.[55] When Constantine died in 775 the

6-2

image-worshippers were cowed but by no means eliminated. The chief political result of Iconoclasm had been the loss of Byzantine Italy to the Lombards. The Italians were strongly opposed to the doctrine; and the Papacy, while still nominally deferential to the Emperor, was not going now to do anything to help him.[56]

Constantine's son, Leo IV, under the influence of the Patriarch and of his Athenian-born Empress, Irene, at first followed a mild policy. He tried to reconcile the monasteries by appointing monks to bishoprics, and he re-introduced the practice of sending disgraced ministers into monasteries. But when Nicetas died in 780 and was succeeded by a sterner Iconoclast, Paul IV, a number of civil servants who were suspected of worshipping images were degraded and tortured, perhaps as a warning to the Empress not to go against official policy. But Leo himself died a few months later, in September 780, leaving the throne to his nine-year-old son and the regency to Irene.[57] She could now set about the restoration of image-worship. Her success was only temporary, in spite of the skill and tact with which she proceeded. The Iconoclastic controversy was to trouble the Empire for another half century. But that she succeeded at all demonstrated that even the Holy Emperor, the Priest-King, as he claimed to be, could not permanently force upon his people a theology that the people disliked.

4

THE WORKING COMPROMISE:
THE LIMITS OF IMPERIAL CONTROL

The Emperor Leo III had introduced Iconoclasm high-handedly, on his own authority. Constantine V, though he had given himself the support of a Council of the Church, had been even more high-handed in enforcing the doctrine. Could it now be abandoned without damaging the prestige of the Imperial office? If a new priest-king were to promulgate a doctrine completely opposed to his predecessors', there must be something wrong with the priesthood. It was, perhaps, fortunate that the ruler who was determined to re-establish image-worship was not a priest-king. The Empress Mother Irene was, as a crowned Augusta, a recognized repository of Imperial power; and no one questioned her right to be Regent for her young son. But as a woman she could not be a priest. Her coronation had not included the element of ordination which a crowned Emperor received. She could not act as Pontifex and make her own pronouncements on theology, nor could the child-Emperor, her son. So, if she were to alter the religious policy of the Empire, she had to operate through the

Church. The Church thereby to some extent won
a constitutional victory, but it was won at the expense
of a woman Regent, not of a Holy Emperor.[1]

Irene was devout and genuinely devoted to image-
worship. But she had to act with caution. First, it
was necessary to remove Iconoclastic officials. The
civil service had to learn that preferment now
depended on a proper respect for images. It was
less easy to convince the army that Iconoclasm must
be abandoned. Irene's attempts gradually to replace
Iconoclastic military commanders by her own supporters were not always wise and were resented by
the troops. She never won the confidence of the
army. She had no difficulty in finding sympathetic
churchmen to fill the bishoprics; but the Iconoclastic
Patriarch Paul presented a problem. However, in
784 he fell seriously ill and came to regard his illness
as a divine punishment for his theological errors. Of
his own accord he abdicated. The Empress went to
see him on his sickbed, bringing with her all the
Iconoclastic officials that she could muster, in order
that they might have the edifying experience of
hearing him make his recantation.[2]

As Paul's successor Irene appointed a layman,
Tarasius, head of the Imperial Chancery. He refused
the appointment at first, saying that he had no wish
to head a Church which was in schism with the other
Churches of Christendom. Having thus made it clear
that he intended to abandon Iconoclasm, he was

unanimously elected by the Synod and rushed through the stages of ordination. Amongst the monks there were several who regarded the elevation of a layman as unseemly; but the practice was often to be repeated in later years.[3]

The new Patriarch at once wrote to the Pope and to the Eastern Patriarchs, inviting them to a Council in Constantinople which should regulate the whole question of image-worship; and the Pope was asked to name the date. Pope Hadrian I responded cordially, though he ventured to question the canonicity of Tarasius's elevation and to remind the Patriarch of the illegality of the transfer of the province of Illyricum. It was agreed that the Council should be held in the summer of 786.[4] Unfortunately, while the Court was travelling in Thrace earlier in the summer, a military plot was hatched. When on 17 August the delegates met together for the opening session in the Church of the Holy Apostles, soldiers from the Imperial guard and other regiments broke into the building and threatened to kill anyone who did not leave it at once. The Empress vainly sent ministers to pacify the soldiers. The Council broke up, and the delegates prepared to return home. Irene refused to be defeated. The mutinous soldiers were sent from the capital on the pretext of being needed on the Eastern frontier, and were eventually disarmed and replaced by reliable troops from the European provinces. But it was not till May 787 that she felt able to reconvene the Council.

The Papal delegates were by then on their homeward journey. They were intercepted in Sicily and were brought back to Constantinople. By September all the delegates had returned and the Council was re-opened, not in Constantinople but in the hallowed city of Nicaea, far from the danger of riots. Tarasius presided till the last session, for which the Council was moved to the Magnaura Palace in Constantinople. The Empress and her son were present there and signed the Acts of the Council in purple ink.[5]

Much of the Council's time had been spent in listening to stories of miracles, which were a little irrelevant to its main findings. It drew a distinction between adoration, *latreia*, which could be given to God alone, and veneration, *proskynesis*, which could be given to images of Christ and the saints, as this veneration would pass to the original. The Christology of the *Horos* of 754 was shown to be faulty, for it denied the Incarnation. To say that icon-worship was valueless was to make a Nestorian distinction between the human and the divine. To say that it was idolatrous was to make a Monophysite confusion between them. The Council also ordained that anyone who harmed images or who tried to prevent their worship should be excommunicated. The Roman and Eastern delegates signed the document along with the Byzantine bishops. The Council therefore could legitimately rank as Oecumenical. To the Orthodox it is the Seventh Oecumenical Council. But in fact the Papacy never endorsed its canons, owing to the disapproval of the Carolingian Court.[6]

Having achieved the restoration of image-worship, the Empress and the Patriarch behaved with moderation. Unrepentant Iconoclastic bishops were deprived of their sees but suffered no other punishment. Repentant bishops were not removed, though one or two were temporarily suspended. No other action was taken against the heretics, except that they did not receive promotion at Court. Only the monks, led by the formidable Abbot Platon of Sakkudion and his still more formidable nephew, Theodore, soon to be Abbot of Studion, disapproved. Like the Donatists five centuries earlier, they would not forgive backsliders, Simoniacs who had bought their sees by selling their integrity. They could not forgive Tarasius for his clemency.[7]

Had Irene died soon after the Council of Nicaea she would have been regarded by history as a wise and tactful ruler who had re-introduced image-worship with remarkably little rancour or fuss. The rest of her career was less admirable, owing to her love of power. She was bitterly resentful when her son came of age and wished to take over the government. But he was a foolish boy, with a taste for soldiering but a distaste for administration. He could not manage entirely to exclude her from power. Relations between mother and son worsened, till in August 797 Irene's agents seized him and put out his eyes, thus disqualifying him for the throne. Irene then reigned for five years as sole autocrat. She could claim that the Imperial power rested with her as Augusta until she chose to appoint a new Emperor; and as she did not choose to do so it remained with her. The lawyers accepted this, though the two laws of hers that survive run in the name of 'Irene the pious Emperor'.[8] The Church, especially the monks with their liking for trouble-making, might have been expected to protest that a woman could not be *pontifex*. But the monks were devoted to Irene. Her son had outraged devout society by divorcing the wife that Irene had chosen for him and marrying and crowning his mistress. The Patriarch, Tarasius, refused to perform the marriage ceremony, but he did not excommunicate the priest who performed it, nor the Emperor, as the monks demanded. Irene let it be known that she sympathized with the monks, who therefore welcomed her rule, and, so long as she reigned, respected it by not openly attacking the Patriarch, though they would not communicate with him. But the quarrel, which was known as the Moechian, or 'adulterous', schism, was not healed.[9] Irene's reign was marked by an extravagant fiscal policy and a humiliating foreign policy. Being unable to trust the army, with its Iconoclastic traditions and its contempt for a woman ruler, she was obliged to pay a heavy tribute to the Caliph of Baghdad.[10] A more disastrous outcome of her rule was that in Old Rome the absence of an

Emperor on the throne was noted, and, as New Rome
was doing nothing to fill the vacancy, Pope Leo III
felt himself to be justified in placing an Imperial
crown on the head of Charles, King of the Franks.[11]
Charles himself, much as he desired the Imperial
title, was somewhat embarrassed by the manner in
which he received it and was anxious to legitimate
himself in the eyes of Constantinople, where the
Papal action was angrily resented and never forgiven.
As a solution Charles suggested that he and Irene
should marry. She did not dislike the idea; but before
anything could come of it, she fell from power, in
October 802.[12]

Her successor, Nicephorus I, her former treasurer,
was an able financier and a tolerant theologian. He
offended the monks by holding a Council which
pronounced Constantine VI's adulterous marriage
legal on the grounds that the Emperor could be
dispensed from obeying the laws of the Church.[13]
He was also suspected of protecting heretics.[14] But
his reign might have been successful had he been a
better general. His troops were no match for the
Caliph's in 806. In 811 he marched out against the
aggressive Bulgarian Khan Krum, and was defeated
and slain in a disastrous battle in the Bulgarian
mountains. His son and heir, Stauracius, was
mortally wounded in the battle; and the throne
eventually passed to Michael Rhangabe, who had
married Nicephorus's daughter.[15]

Michael was an amiable man who managed to bring Theodore of Studion, now the leader of the monkish party, and the Patriarch Nicephorus, the historian, who had succeeded Tarasius in 806 and who shared his moderate views, round the same table. The confrontation was not a success. Theodore could not forgive Nicephorus for the Council of 809. Now, when they met, the Patriarch proposed enforcing the death penalty on notorious heretics such as the Paulicians and the Athingani. Theodore protested that it might always be possible to convert them from their errors. Then, when Krum offered peace, on condition that traitor refugees on either side should be extradited for punishment, and the Emperor and Patriarch both favoured acceptance, Theodore declared that it would be sinful to return refugee Bulgarians, many of them now converts to Christianity, to certain death. His view prevailed. The war was resumed; and Michael was severely beaten by Krum at Vernisicia in the spring of 813.[16]

The Moechian schism weakened the image-worshipping party. And now, after these military disasters, men remembered with nostalgia the great soldier-emperors of the Iconoclastic Isaurian dynasty. Consequently, when the army revolted against Michael's incompetence and marched on the capital, no one openly objected when it placed its leading general, Leo the Armenian, on the throne.[17]

Leo V was an iconoclast, as befitted a soldier from

the eastern provinces. He waited until the Bulgarian menace had been removed by the death of Krum in April 814. Then, that autumn, he appointed a mixed committee of churchmen and scholars who shared his views, the most brilliant being a young Armenian philosopher called John the Grammarian, to collect arguments and texts in support of Iconoclasm. They produced a *florilegium*, which the Emperor handed to the Patriarch, declaring the people were offended by images, strengthening his argument by encouraging soldiers to mutilate the image of Christ over the Palace gate, which Irene had replaced. On Christmas Eve, 814, the Patriarch read out the *florilegium* to an assembly of bishops and abbots, the vast majority of whom agreed with him that it was unacceptable. On Christmas Day the Emperor, after attending the dawn service in Saint Sophia, where he was seen to make obeisance before an icon of Christ, summoned the Patriarch and his assembly to the Palace. He opened the meeting by saying that a number of scholars and theologians were questioning the propriety of image-worship and their views should be heard. It was his duty, he said, not to remain silent concerning a religious inquiry. If it was a religious inquiry, asked the Bishop of Cyzicus, why was it not held in a church but in the Palace? The Emperor replied that it was his duty to act as mediator. Why, then, asked the Bishop of Synnada, was he encouraging their opponents and sheltering them in the Palace?

This was tyranny, not mediation. Other bishops raised theological arguments. The Emperor pretended to be a neutral judge, till at last Theodore of Studion cried out: 'Do not undo the status of the Church; for the Apostle said: "He gave some, apostles; and some, prophets; and some, evangelists; and some, pastors and teachers, for the perfecting of the Faith." But he did not mention Emperors. To you, Emperor, has been entrusted the political government and the army. Look after them, and leave the Church to its shepherds and teachers, as the Apostle ordained.'[18]

Such a confrontation would have been impossible in the days of the great Justinian or even in those of Leo III. Never before had the ecclesiastical authority of the Emperor been so brusquely challenged to his face. But Leo V was not to be deflected. The Patriarch Nicephorus abdicated with dignity and retired to a monastery, where he wrote treatises against Iconoclasm.[19] Theodore of Studion was exiled, and in exile he too wrote against the heresy and, more passionately, against the Emperor's interference in Church affairs. His view was that the power to bind and loose had been given to the holders of the five Patriarchal sees. They formed 'the court of judgment as regards divine doctrine. To kings and rulers', he adds, 'it appertains only to provide aid, to join in attesting the faith, and to deal with secular affairs. Nothing else has been given to them by God in respect to divine doctrines.'[20] He wrote on several occasions to the Pope, calling him the 'chief holder of the keys of heaven': though when the Pope disappointed him, his comment was: 'What do we care if the Pope acts in one way or another?'[21] But he did care that the Church should not be submitted to the whims of the Emperor. He did not succeed in his efforts for the full independence of the Church; but those efforts undoubtedly succeeded in placing a limit on the divine authority of the Emperor.

At Easter, 815, the Emperor summoned a Council of the Church to meet in Saint Sophia. By now he had appointed a number of Iconoclastic bishops; and there were shameful scenes when the image-worshipping bishops were insulted and manhandled. The Council annulled the canons of the Council of Nicaea and confirmed those of the Council of 754.[22] There followed a period of persecution, in which the Studites and their followers were the main victims. Many were imprisoned or exiled, and some were tortured, though it seems that no one was put to death. This continued for five years, till Christmas Day 820, when, to Theodore of Studion's unconcealed delight, the Emperor Leo was brutally murdered in church by his aide-de-camp, Michael the Amorian, who seized the throne.[23]

Michael II had Iconoclastic sympathies, but he practised tolerance, partly out of a lack of interest in religion, a rare trait in a Byzantine Emperor, and partly because for two years he had to fight his old comrade and rival, Thomas the Slav, in order to keep the throne, and he could not afford to antagonize large sections of the people. He recalled the exiled monks; and images were permitted to hang in churches except in Constantinople. The only image-worshipper to suffer ill treatment during the reign was the monk Methodius, who had fled to Rome as a refugee during Leo V's reign and returned to Constantinople in 821 with a letter from Pope Paschal I, ordering the Emperor to restore the true faith. Michael was annoyed by the tone of the letter and sentenced Methodius to be scourged and imprisoned as a traitor. But, though it was known that Methodius had been inspired by the Studites, no action was taken against them, while Methodius himself soon became an intimate friend of the Imperial family.[24] Michael attempted to restore unity with the Western Church by negotiating with the Western Emperor, Louis the Pious: who in 825 obliged Pope Paschal to approve of the findings of a Council held at Paris, which maintained that images could hang in churches but must not be paid any form of worship. The compromise fitted in with Michael's tastes, but it was soon forgotten in the West.[25] Michael further offended the Studites by marrying a nun as his second wife. It was a politic marriage, for the bride was Euphrosyne, only surviving daughter of Constantine VI and granddaughter of Irene. The Patriarch Antony I, a keen but tolerant Iconoclast, gladly gave the necessary dispensation; and public opinion, in spite of the Studites, seems to have been untroubled. It was a childless marriage; and as soon as she was widowed Euphrosyne returned happily to her convent.[26]

Michael II's son, Theophilus, who was autocrat from 829 to 842, was personally an Iconoclast but, like his father, tolerant. Indeed, it would have been difficult for him to persecute image-worshippers, as his wife, Theodora, to whom he was devoted, was notoriously of their number. In any case, Iconoclasm had now largely altered its complexion. Under the Isaurian Emperors it had been a stern austere movement, disliking not only images but all the rich trappings of the churches. Now the leading Iconoclasts were men like John the Grammarian and Theophilus himself, intellectuals with a taste for classical learning and the arts, whose dislike of images was partly philosophical but still more based on their dislike of the monks, who now, ironically, represented the stern Protestant party in the Church, and obscurantism in education. Theophilus was a great ruler. Even his enemies admitted that never for centuries had justice been so fairly administered, nor the economy so well run, nor had the prestige of the Empire stood so high. He was a great builder, and he and his Court did everything to encourage intellectual and artistic life. In so doing Theophilus unintentionally helped to destroy Iconoclasm. He forbade religious painting. Churches were decorated with animals and birds, fishes and flowers, to look like a zoological garden, one writer of the time complained.[27] But the artists whom he patronized were sooner or later going to insist on their right to paint religious themes if they so wished; nor were intellectual circles going to be restricted in their reading of the Fathers of the Church when those whom they admired the most for their philosophy and their style were Fathers such as the Cappadocians, whose Neoplatonic traditions approved of images. By the middle of the ninth century intellectual circles, while remaining opposed to the monkish party, were moving over away from Iconoclasm.[28]

When Theophilus died in January 842, leaving a two-year-old son, Michael III, to succeed him, the regency passed to his widow, Theodora. She, like the last Empress-Regent, Irene, was determined to restore image-worship, but, like Irene, she saw that she must move cautiously. She waited until she could convince her chief minister Theoctistus, an able man who had risen to power under Theophilus, that the people in general would welcome the change, and until she was herself assured that her late husband would not be anathematized. In March 843 she summoned a Council to meet in the Palace precincts. The bishops willingly re-affirmed the canons of the Council of Nicaea, the only eminent dissentient being the Patriarch, the scholar John the Grammarian. He was deposed and retired to study necromancy in his villa on the Bosphorus. In his place Theodora told the Council to elect Methodius, the monk who had offended Michael II twenty years before and had since become a close friend of Theophilus. Like the Patriarch Tarasius half a century earlier, Methodius showed great moderation. The only bishops to lose their sees were those who refused any form of compromise. There was no persecution. No anathemas were pronounced against distinguished Iconoclasts. It seems, too, that the authorities waited for some twenty years before re-introducing figure-mosaics into such great public monuments as Saint Sophia. Peace was restored to the Church, to the satisfaction of everyone except for a few extremist monks who felt that the Iconoclasts had not been properly punished. But even the monks could hardly disapprove of the pious Empress who had given them back their images.[29]

Theodora had been even more successful than Irene in restoring images without damaging the prestige of the Imperial throne. But soon the relations between Patriarch and Emperor were to be troubled again. When Methodius died in 847 Theodora appointed as his successor a monk, Ignatius, who was the son of Michael I Rhangabe, and had been castrated when his father lost the throne. He had become a monk and in time abbot of a monastery in the Princes' Islands, and was highly esteemed for his piety and his charity. The Empress doubtless hoped that with his distinguished background he would have a statesman-like vision. She was wrong. Ignatius was committed to the extreme monastic party. Trouble began at his enthronization, when he refused to receive the Archbishop of Syracuse, Gregory Asbestas, accusing him of uncanonical behaviour. It is probable that the Archbishop, who had been a friend of Methodius, was already organizing an opposition party against the new Patriarch. The Archbishop informed the Pope, Leo IV, who considered that Syracuse, being in Sicily, came under his jurisdiction, and sent to Constantinople to demand an explanation. He received no satisfaction; nor did his successor, Benedict III, who announced that the Archbishop could not be deposed until Rome had investigated the matter. Ignatius ignored the Papal demands. Relations between the Papacy and the Patriarchate were suspended.[30]

In 856 Theodora was removed from the regency by her brother Bardas, acting in the name of the Emperor Michael III, now aged sixteen; Bardas took over the government, with the title of Caesar. He was a brilliant ruler. He revitalized the army and the navy; he refounded the University; he inaugurated the missionary venture that was to convert the Slavs and arranged the conversion of Bulgaria. But he had enemies, civil servants who resented his squandering of the reserves that his sister had accumulated, and churchmen, especially the monks, who disapproved of his private life. Ignatius offended him first by refusing to send Theodora against her will into a convent, and then, irreparably, in 858 by accusing him of adulterous relations with his daughter-in-law and excommunicating him. The accusation may have been false; but Bardas's reputation for immorality and for encouraging his nephew's immorality was so notorious that he did not dare to protest. Instead, he trumped up a charge of treason against both Theodora and Ignatius. Theodora was now forced into a convent and Ignatius deposed on Imperial orders by the Holy Synod.[31]

To succeed Ignatius Bardas saw to the appointment of the most distinguished scholar of the time, Photius. Photius was the great-nephew of Tarasius, and, like Tarasius, was head of the Imperial Chancery when he was appointed Patriarch, and, like him too, had to be rushed through the stages of ordination. He was enthroned on Christmas Day 858. The monkish party, despite Ignatius's bad relations with Rome, decided to appeal to the Pope, Nicholas I, against his appointment. Nicholas was delighted with the chance of intervention, but he made any chance of a peaceful solution impossible by raising the question of the jurisdiction over the province of Illyricum, now politically very important because it contained the Kingdom of Bulgaria, newly converted to Christianity. It is irrelevant to our theme to describe how Photius won over the Papal delegates and outwitted the Papacy both over his own position and over the question of the Bulgarian Church, and how he drove a wedge between Rome and the monastic party in Byzantium which had hitherto been so eager to appeal to Rome. The relevant point is that Photius could only carry out his schemes so long as he enjoyed Imperial support. When in April 866 his patron, the Caesar Bardas, was ousted and murdered by Michael III's new favourite, the ex-groom, Basil the Macedonian, Photius's embarrassed attempt to condone the murder did not help him. In September 867, Michael III was murdered by Basil's minions, and Basil became autocrat. Almost his first act was to have Photius deposed and Ignatius re-instated as Patriarch. The Papacy was delighted, until it discovered that Ignatius, under Basil's direction, was as unwilling as Photius to let it interfere in Byzantine or Bulgarian affairs. Meanwhile Photius, after a short period in exile, managed to win Basil's goodwill. He was made Rector of the University and tutor to the Emperor's heir, Leo VI. When Ignatius died in 877, Photius returned, fully rehabilitated, to the Patriarchal throne.[32]

Photius was an efficient Patriarch whose work in reforming the Patriarchal school was especially valuable. But his ambition was growing. When in 881 the Emperor Basil began to suffer from bouts of madness, Photius, who seems to have poisoned Basil's mind against his son Leo, virtually took over the government. He relished his power. Basil had commissioned a new summarized law-code, the *Epanagoge*, for which Photius drafted the preface. In it, while declaring, as Justinian and Leo III had done in their time, that 'the peace and prosperity of the citizens, in body and soul, depends on the concord of the kingship and the priesthood', he gives no precedence to the kingship. He raises the Patriarch to be in effect the equal partner of the Emperor. He is 'the animate and living image of Christ'. He alone can interpret the canons of the Church and the decrees of the Councils. These are words more suited to a Roman pontiff than to a Byzantine prelate.[33] In the outcome the *Epanagoge* was never officially issued; and Photius's pride was soon to be humbled. When Leo VI succeeded his father in 885, he at once accused Photius of treason. After an inquiry lasting for several months the Patriarch was deposed and exiled. Leo then appointed as Patriarch his nineteen-year-old brother, Stephen. It seems that Basil had planned the appointment, believing that only a reliable member of the Imperial family on the Patriarchal throne could prevent such episodes as the dispute between Ignatius and Photius. Public opinion seems to have accepted the boy-prince's elevation without demur. The monkish party was probably too happy at the fall of Photius, whom it detested, to make any protest.[34]

Stephen might have been an excellent Patriarch.

But he wore himself out by his ascetic life and died aged twenty-three. Leo then appointed a respectable and moderate cleric, Antony II Cauleas, who on his orders summoned a Synod, attended by delegates from Rome, at which the schism caused by Photius and Ignatius was declared to be closed, neither protagonist being condemned.[35] When Antony died in 901, his successor was the Imperial Secretary, or *Mysticus*, Nicholas. Nicholas was the son of an Italian slave-woman working in the household of Photius's family. His career shows that humble birth was no bar to advancement in Byzantium. Photius had been struck by the boy's brains and had seen to his education. Nicholas had become a close friend of the Emperor, who felt that he could trust him. He was in fact an ambitious and obstinate man; but he was very ready to work in with Leo. Fate decided otherwise.[36]

Marriage in Byzantium was an affair for the civil courts, though it required the blessing of the Church. But religious opinion had long thought that Roman civil law was lax on the subject, particularly on the question how many times re-marriage was lawful. Many Christian writers had held stern views. Saint Basil, for instance, only allowed a second marriage subject to a penance. He considered a third marriage to be 'moderated fornication', to be punished by excommunication for four years, though the issue would be legitimate. A fourth marriage was sheer bestiality.[37] In the 870s a law was published in the name of Basil I and his sons Constantine (who died in 879) and Leo, which bowed to public opinion and permitted a third marriage only with a special dispensation and absolutely forbidding a fourth marriage, which would be invalid and its issue illegitimate.[38]

Leo had been married when young by his father to a saintly but doubtless unattractive woman called Theophano, whom he disliked. The marriage lasted for eleven years until she died, utterly neglected, in 897. Leo had meanwhile enjoyed the embraces of a lady of negro origin, Zoe, daughter of Zaoutzes.[39] She bore him a daughter, Anna. Within a few months of Theophano's death Leo married Zoe, thus legitimizing the child. But Zoe died in 899, without further issue. The only male member of the Imperial family, apart from the Emperor, was now his youngest brother, Alexander, a dissolute youth who also was childless. So in 900 Leo received a dispensation to marry again; but his new Empress died in April 901, after giving birth to a son who survived only a few days. It was inconvenient for the Court to be without an Empress. So Leo crowned his young daughter Augusta, perhaps intending that she and her future husband should succeed him. But he had plans to marry her to a Western prince; and, anyhow, she was soon to die. How was the dynasty to be perpetuated? Leo decided to take an official mistress, Zoe, called Carbopsina, the dark-eyed, a lady of good family. In 903 or 904 Zoe bore a daughter, who also died young. Then, in September 905, she bore a son, Constantine, surnamed Porphyrogenitus, as he was born in the purple chamber reserved for the birth of Imperial children. But, in spite of his birth-place, he was a bastard. The Patriarch Nicholas agreed to baptize him, but only if the Imperial mistress was dismissed from the Court. But that was not enough for Leo. To legitimize the boy he must marry his mother. The marriage was performed by a com-plaisant priest in April 906, without the Patriarch's knowledge; and Zoe was simultaneously crowned Empress.[40]

Leo had broken a law that he himself had pro-mulgated. Pious opinion was deeply shocked. In particular the monks, who still felt indignation about the adulterous marriage of Constantine VI a century earlier, did not hide their sense of outrage. The Patriarch, who, as a pupil of Photius, did not approve of the monkish party, had, it seems, been prepared to make use of 'economy', the principle that a dis-pensation from canon law can be allowed in special circumstances provided that no essential article of faith was involved, but only so far as to legitimize the child. But, like Photius, he was anxious to assert the moral authority of the Patriarchate; and Leo had tricked him over the marriage. He might still have been ready to make some compromise. But within his own Photian party he had a rival, Arethas, Archbishop of Caesarea, a man of great learning and few scruples, who, more to embarrass Nicholas than from conviction, now allied himself with the monastic party and stirred up public opinion against any idea of a dispensation. The strength of the feeling that was aroused, combined with his own anger against the unrepentant Emperor, forced him to take action. On Christmas Day 906 he closed the doors of the Church of Saint Sophia in the Emperor's face. But Leo outwitted him. He had already sent in secret envoys to the Pope and to the Eastern Patriarchs to ask for their views on fourth marriages, in the knowledge that in the West there was no limit on re-marriage, while the Eastern Patriarchs, eager for subsidies and for diplomatic support, would always support the Emperor. All were naturally delighted to prove the Patriarch of Constantinople to be in error. As soon as Leo heard that the answer from Rome was on its way he arrested Nicholas and forced him to abdicate. Then he approached the monkish party, knowing that with its Studite traditions it could not but approve of appeals to Rome and to the other great Churches. The most eminent monkish leader was a saintly monk, Euthymius, whom Leo had sometimes consulted on spiritual matters. Fortified by the approval of the Universal Church he agreed to accept the Patriarchate and to give the Emperor a dispensation which would condone the fourth marriage. His acceptance made havoc of the old party alignment.

Many of the monks now transferred their allegiance to Nicholas, while Arethas of Caesarea and many of the Court clergy became ardent supporters of Euthymius and of fourth marriages.[41]

Leo's health began to fail early in 912; and in April that year, when he was obviously dying, his brother Alexander, who had been co-Emperor but excluded from power for many years, took over the government, the young Constantine, who had been crowned co-Emperor in 911, being not yet seven years old. Leo died in May; but already Alexander had dismissed Euthymius, who was cruelly insulted and manhandled by his police. Nicholas was reinstated, and tried to regain control of the Church by degrading all bishops consecrated by Euthymius and all other hierarchs known to support him. But, headed by Arethas of Caesarea, many of them refused to leave their sees. The turmoil in the Church increased and was worsened by Nicholas's severance of relations with Rome. But Nicholas's patron, Alexander, died in May 912, leaving the government in the hands of a Regency Council of which Nicholas was president. Nicholas enjoyed his power. He suppressed a revolt which he was suspected of having at first encouraged. He negotiated on his own with the Bulgarian monarch, Symeon, even crowning him with an improvised crown and promising that the young Emperor Constantine should marry his daughter. In eight months he made himself thoroughly unpopular. No Byzantine, whatever his views about the Patriarchate, liked to see a priest exercising secular power. In February 914 a plot easily ousted him from the government; and the regency passed to the Emperor's mother, the dark-eyed Zoe. She wished to restore Euthymius to the Patriarchate; but he refused the uncomfortable chair. So she grudgingly retained Nicholas, telling him to restrict himself to Church affairs.[42]

After a good beginning Zoe's regency collapsed in 919, in the course of a disastrous war against the Bulgarians.[43] The Grand Admiral, Romanus Lecapenus, seized power, married the young Emperor to his daughter, and made himself Basileopator, 'the Emperor's father', then Caesar and ultimately Emperor. He kept Nicholas strictly under control, though he sometimes made use of his diplomatic experience. In 920 a Council was held to unite the Church. Its findings, which were published in a *Tomus Unionis*, gave control over the marriage laws to the Church, condemned fourth marriages and even queried the propriety of third marriages. But 'economy' was used to legitimize the position of the young Emperor Constantine and to justify the Euthymian clergy who had condoned Leo's fourth marriage. In 923 Nicholas made his peace with Rome, declaring, without any proof, that the Pope had signified his adherence to the *Tomus Unionis*.[44]

The *Tetragamia*, this affair of the fourth marriage,

had created the most dangerous crisis between Emperor and Patriarch in the middle Byzantine period. It resulted in a slight limitation of the Emperor's power. Leo had been morally and legally in the wrong. He had performed an act repugnant to pious sentiment and had broken his own law in so doing. The *Tomus Unionis* showed that the Emperor could not flout the law on what was now recognized to be a religious matter, but 'economy' could be applied by the Church to excuse him in special circumstances. Byzantine public opinion was not wholly consistent. It allowed the Emperor to make and unmake Patriarchs; but, unless his moral position was sure, he would cause a schism by such action. It supported a Patriarch who opposed the Emperor on moral grounds, but not a Patriarch who attempted to govern the State, even though the task was be-queathed to him by Imperial authority. Leo succeeded in his main object, which was to establish his dynasty. Constantine, the baby whose legitimacy was at stake, was never regarded as being other than a lawful Emperor. Even the usurper Romanus Lecapenus dared not disregard his ultimate right to the autocracy. The Imperial family was more deeply grounded in public affection than any Patriarch, however formid-able his authority.

Romanus Lecapenus, like Leo VI, decided to make one of his family Patriarch. When Nicholas died in 925, the prince whom he had chosen, his youngest son Theophylact, was still too young. Two stop-gap Patriarchs were appointed till Theophylact succeeded in 931, at the age of not quite fifteen. No one seems to have protested against the appointment. The Pope, John XI, even sent his blessing; but it must be admitted that John XI was in the power of his half-brother, Alberic, Prince of the Romans, who wanted the alliance of the Emperor. Theophylact was an amiable youth who was only interested in breeding horses. As a Patriarch he was inoffensive. He died in 956.[45]

The experiment of a Prince-Patriarch was not repeated. As Theophylact's successor Constantine VII, now at last sole autocrat, selected a monk, Polyeuct. It was a mistake. Polyeuct was only happy when he could protest. He protested against the actions and the morals of ministers. He protested against the terms of the *Tomus Unionis*. Constantine VII was exasperated, but died before he could depose him.[46] When Constantine's son, Romanus II, died in 963, leaving two small sons, Basil II and Constantine VIII, as Emperors under the regency of their mother Theophano, and when Theophano decided to marry the great general Nicephorus Phocas and raise him to the autocracy, Polyeuct protested, asserting incorrectly that they were spiritually related.[47] He protested, with better cause and more success, when Nicephorus wished him to give the status of martyr to any soldier who fell fighting against the infidel.[48]

He came into his own in 969, when Nicephorus was murdered by John Tzimisces, his nephew, who then wished to marry the Empress Theophano, his partner in the crime. Polyeuct refused to crown John Emperor unless he abandoned Theophano, whose third husband he would have been, and unless he undertook to rescind Nicephorus's legislation against the monasteries and, it was said, acknowledge the Patriarch as supreme master in all ecclesiastical affairs.[49] Had John not been an usurper and a murderer, he could have removed the Patriarch and appointed a more subservient substitute. But in his weak position he needed Polyeuct's help. The triumph of the Patriarchate was short-lived. When the tiresome Polyeuct died the following year John elevated a saintly monk to the Patriarchate. The speech with which he announced the appointment has survived. In it the Emperor talked of the two powers, the priesthood and the kingship, but he made their relationship clear when he went on to say that as the head of the priesthood was dead, he on his Imperial authority was placing on the ecclesiastical throne a man whom he judged to be worthy.[50]

For the next seventy years no Patriarch attempted to challenge Imperial authority. It would have needed a bold cleric to oppose the Emperor Basil II, who kept the Patriarchate vacant for nearly five years after the death of Nicholas II Chrysoberges, it seems because Nicholas had tried to extract from him tax-concessions for the Church at a moment when the Emperor was distracted by civil war. When towards the end of Basil's reign the Patriarch Sergius II ventured to complain about the taxation of Church estates, his complaints were disregarded.[51]

A few days before Basil II died, in December 1025, he appointed as Patriarch Alexius, Abbot of Studion, who was to prove a good friend to the dynasty. He gave valuable support to Basil's niece, the Empress Zoe, in 1043, when her adopted son, Michael V, attempted to send her into exile.[52] When he died the following year, Zoe's third husband, Constantine IX, unwisely chose as his successor a scholar-diplomat, Michael Cerularius, who had become a monk to avoid further punishment after having been involved in a plot against Michael IV. Cerularius was an ambitious man; and Constantine's weak character gave him his chance. It was a time when reforms in the Western Church were giving to the Roman Pope a supreme and centralized control over it all, and the temporary weakness of the Western Emperors, who had inaugurated the reforms, was enabling the Papacy to cast off secular control. Cerularius was aware of these developments and wished to raise his Patriarchate into a similar position. But if the Patriarchate of Constantinople was to become an Eastern equivalent of the Papacy, it must be completely independent of the Papacy, as well as of Imperial domination. The liking of the monkish party in Byzantium to make appeals to Rome against the Byzantine hierarchy had faded, chiefly as a result of the affair of the *Tetragamia*, but partly, too, owing to the revival of the Western Empire under the Ottos and to the new aggressive claims of the Papacy, which realized that if its supremacy over Christendom was to be complete, it must include supremacy over the Churches of the East as well as of the West. The average Byzantine now regarded Rome as a small provincial city with a great past and an insignificant present, and its Church as a once great institution which was now in the hands of barbarians. An attack on Roman pretensions would be popular in Constantinople. But there was a counter-theme. The Byzantine provinces in southern Italy were now being overrun by Norman invaders, whose lawless activities were equally worrying to the Pope, as they threatened his own territory. It was therefore the Emperor's policy to co-operate with the Pope, who might in addition be able to use his religious authority to restrain the Normans.

Cerularius put an end to that policy. It may have been his determination to bring the Armenian Church into conformity with the Byzantine which drew his attention to certain religious practices which the Armenians shared with the Romans and of which he did not approve. In 1052, on his sole authority, he ordered the closure of all Latin churches within his Patriarchate. These included the Church of the

Varangian Guard in Constantinople, the churches of the Amalfitans and other Italian merchant communities there and in the other cities of the Empire, and, he intended, Latin churches in Byzantine Italy. He then induced Leo, Metropolitan of Ochrida, to write a letter to the Bishop of Trani, chief Orthodox ecclesiastic in southern Italy, denouncing various Roman practices, in particular the use of unleavened bread at the Sacrament. The bishop was told to circulate the letter round Italy.

All this was done without the permission of the Emperor. The political situation in Italy was tense at the moment, Pope Leo IX having just been made prisoner by the Normans, with whom he was negotiating for his release. Constantine IX hastened to write a cordial letter to the Pope, suggesting further consultation; and he persuaded Cerularius to write to him too, suggesting that they should discuss the ecclesiastical position. Leo IX responded by sending legates to Constantinople to deal with both the political and the religious issues. The Emperor received them with honour. Unfortunately, the chief Roman legate, Cardinal Humbert, was a truculent man who had himself written a tract against Greek 'errors'. He was not prepared to make friends with the Patriarch, who was equally determined to be intransigent, and whose propaganda in Constantinople was very efficient. The Papal mission was made to appear as an attempt by coarse foreigners to dictate

8-2

to the Byzantines about their faith and their liturgy. In this atmosphere the Emperor's efforts to smoothe things over came to nothing. At last, after mutual insults, Humbert, whose legatine authority had actually lapsed, Pope Leo having died in April 1054, stalked into the Church of Saint Sophia on the afternoon of 16 July 1054, and laid on the altar a bull of excommunication against the Patriarch, a verbose, offensive and inaccurate document, which shocked even the Emperor. Cerularius replied by excommunicating Humbert. The 'schism' of 1054 was thus merely a case of two hierarchs personally excommunicating each other. But in fact, in spite of earnest attempts at reconciliation, good relations between the Churches of Rome and Constantinople were never to be restored.[53]

The episode showed that where politics were immingled with a religious issue a Patriarch who was sure of popular support could defy the Emperor and ruin Imperial policy. But, like the Patriarch Nicholas Mysticus, Cerularius found that when he tried to interfere in purely political matters he lost popular support. Constantine IX remained in awe of him; but when he attempted to dictate to Constantine's successor, the aged spinster Theodora, last of the Macedonian line, she told him to keep to Church affairs. The next Emperor, Michael VI, tried to follow her example; but he was a feeble old man, without the prestige that she inherited. Cerularius showed his contempt for him by assuming the purple footwear reserved for Emperors, and by joining in the plot to replace him by the soldier, Isaac Comnenus. In return Isaac, when once on the throne, rewarded Cerularius by giving to the Patriarchate complete control over the Imperial Cathedral of Saint Sophia; but he soon was exasperated by the Patriarch's arrogance and took steps to depose him, with popular opinion now on his side. When Cerularius heard of this his rage brought on an apoplectic fit, of which he died.[54]

The career of Cerularius showed both the power and the limitations of the Patriarchate. The lesson was learnt on both sides. Two centuries were to pass before there was another crisis between Emperor and Patriarchate in Byzantium.

5

THE MONKS AND THE PEOPLE:
THE OPPOSITION TO THE
PALACE AND THE HIERARCHY

In the course of Byzantine history we meet from
time to time a politico-religious party based on the
monasteries. Even in the fifth century monastic communities such as that of Sosthenion in Constantinople
exercised an influence on public affairs. But it was
by their leadership in the struggle against Iconoclasm
that the monks came to form a cohesive party which
thenceforward was a powerful element in Byzantine
life. At times this party found support in the Imperial
Court. At times the Patriarch might be chosen from
amongst its ranks. But for most of the time it was
in opposition not only to any Imperial control of the
Church but also to the upper hierarchy, which it
considered to be over-worldly. Its strength lay in its
close touch with public opinion.

It was characteristic of the Byzantines that, while
they deeply respected the Imperium and the Patriarchate as institutions, they were far more deeply
influenced in their ideas and their outlook by the
monks and holy men who moved amongst them. The
Emperor from the very nature of his position was

required to be a somewhat remote figure. The Viceroy of God had to know his place, which was an exalted one. The Emperor should indeed be gracious and affable when he appeared in public. He should be generous and benevolent and should give kindly attention to suppliants who appealed to his justice or to his charity. He should be humble before God. But the idea, so popular nowadays, that the ruler should be chatty and informal with the man in the street was repugnant to the Byzantine sense of propriety and religion.[1] An Emperor who, like Michael III, tried to move on familiar terms amongst his subjects merely embarrassed them and was disliked for it.[2] Similarly, the Patriarch, though he did not enjoy quite the same mystical prestige, should behave as a venerable figure. Respect for the divine authority of Emperor or Patriarch did not prevent the Byzantines from rising in rebellion against a man whom they felt to be unworthy of such a position. But they were rebelling against the human being, not against his sacred role. Indeed, they were rebelling to maintain the standards of his role.

But the loftiness of his position made it difficult for the Emperor to communicate with his subjects. In the days before printing-presses there could be no news-sheets; and even edicts and rescripts could only have a limited circulation, owing to the difficulty of having many copies made. Notices could be posted on the walls of the city streets. Pamphlets could be

handed round the limited circles of the Court and
the bureaucracy and, rather more widely, through
the ecclesiastical organization. But propaganda had
to be spread almost entirely by word of mouth. The
Emperor did not make speeches in public, except
when on certain feast-days it was his right to preach
a sermon in Saint Sophia; and the sermon usually
consisted of pious platitudes.[3] He would occasionally
address the Senate, which had become an amorphous
body of officials and members of the leading families.
But if he wished to explain his policies to the people
in general he would have to send round officials to
talk to the headmen in the various quarters of the
cities and in the villages, as Constantine V did when he
wished to gain support for his Iconoclastic intentions.[4]
Government officials were seldom welcome, as they
were associated with tax-collectors. On a purely
religious matter he could act through the bishops,
ordering them to preach sermons in favour of his
policies and to see that their priests did likewise.
But the priests – and even, at times, the bishops – were
not always willing to carry out instructions of which
they disapproved; and it was not always wise or
popular to dismiss them for such disobedience.[5]

There was, however, a section of the community
which was in a position to go round the homes of
the people in the towns and the villages, telling them
how to behave and what to think. These were the
monks. Byzantine monasticism, unlike that of Western

Europe, had no fixed Rule and no Orders. Each monastery had its own constitution, usually laid down when it was founded and reflecting the intentions of the founder, who was often a layman or a laywoman. Christian monasticism had its origin in the Egyptian desert, to which, in the early centuries of the Church, ascetic men and women would retire to lead lives of holy and humble contemplation. They were the *monachi*, the solitary ones. As time went on these hermits tended to gather together into small groups, for mutual protection and to perform mutual services. The group came to be called a *lavra*. It was loosely organized, without fixed rules. The sexes were not necessarily segregated; and the authority of the abbot was undefined. In the fifth century Saint Basil of Caesarea suggested reforms, in order to make monastic life more orderly and more effective. He held that the monks should live in communities where everything should be held in common and everyone should obey the rule of an elected superior. Everyone should work and perform social services as well as pray.[6]

Thenceforward Basilian, or coenobitic, monasteries were founded in increasing numbers, some still in the depths of the country but others near or even inside cities, where social duties could be performed more effectively. Justinian I used his Imperial authority to legislate on monasteries, passing laws to give them some uniformity. All monasteries were to follow the Basilian pattern. Monks were to dispose of all their property before they entered the monastery, where they were to live a purely communal life. Anyone could become a monk, or a nun, at any age, unless he were a runaway slave or a government official who had not completed his term of office. A married man had to obtain his wife's consent, and a wife her husband's. In such cases it was usual for both of them to take vows simultaneously. He, or she, must pass all his property to his lawful heirs before taking the final vows. The noviciate lasted for three years before the final vows of chastity, poverty and obedience were taken.[7]

The abbot, called either the *higumene*, the leader, or the *archimandrite*, the head of the flock, was elected by a majority vote of the monks; but his election had to be confirmed by the local bishop. When a new monastery was to be founded, the bishop inspected and blessed the site and approved the title-deeds. After that, the monasteries were entirely self-governing, with the abbot in complete authority, so long as he fulfilled the requirements of the title-deeds. There were two deeds: the *brevion*, which listed the endowments and the liturgical duties requested by the founder, and the *typicon*, which listed the special rights and obligations of the monks. The monastery might be required to run an orphanage or a school or a hospital, or to provide a chaplain for the founder's household. Only a small proportion of the monks were priests, but if the abbot were not a priest at the time of his election he had to be ordained; and there had to be a sufficient number of priests in the monastery for the chapel services to be conducted regularly. The abbot was assisted administratively by the *oeconomos*, who looked after the worldly possessions of the monastery, the *chartophylax*, who acted as registrar, and the *bibliophylax*, the librarian – for every monastery was required to contain a library. In the women's establishments the abbess was similarly in complete control, with similar assistance: though chaplains were provided by the bishop to conduct the chapel services.[8]

The bishop retained authority over the external relations of the monastery; and he could intervene were there a grave scandal within its walls or were the abbot to quarrel with his monks. In some establishments the right to intervention belonged not to the local bishop but to the Patriarch, either because they were Patriarchal foundations or because the founder so ordained. Imperial foundations were under the control of the Imperial authorities, the hierarchy having no right to intervene. Later, there were establishments known as *autodespotai*, which by Imperial decree were entirely freed from external control: though in a case of serious crisis or scandal the Emperor would personally inquire into it.[9]

In spite of Justinian's legislation, which was repeated by Justinian II after the Council *in Trullo*, where certain amendments, such as a four-year noviciate, were introduced, the pre-Basilian *lavra* continued to exist in remoter parts of the Empire; and no great efforts were made to suppress it.[10] Moreover, the authorities themselves often broke the law with regard to the noviciate. By the seventh century it was becoming customary to relegate fallen princes and statesmen to monasteries, where they could repent at leisure of their misdeeds and from which they could not hope to re-emerge into secular public life. In such cases there was no time for a noviciate. Vows had to be taken and tonsure performed without any delay. Then there were occasions when the Imperial authorities wished to elevate a layman to the Patriarchate. Tarasius, appointed by Irene, was the first example. It was by then customary that the hierarchy should be filled by men who had taken monastic vows. It was thus necessary for the Patriarch-elect to be rushed through the vows as well as the stages of ordination as quickly as possible.[11]

The fact that bishops came to be chosen only from the ranks of the monks naturally added to the prestige of monasticism. The parish priest, then as now in the Orthodox Church, was a simple man, differing from his fellow-parishioners only in that he was a little better educated and was trained and ordained to perform the sacred Mysteries. He had to be a married man, though he could continue as a priest were his wife to die. He could never expect advancement. In the cities the larger and more fashionable churches were usually attached to monasteries, which provided the chaplains for them. The great cathedrals of Saint Sophia and the Holy Apostles seem to have contained a few secular priests; but they were mainly served by chaplains from the Patriarchal Court, men who had taken monastic vows but were no longer connected with a specific monastery.[12] It was by entering a monastery that an able and ambitious boy could best make a career for himself. Byzantine society was formal but it was never exclusive. It was certainly advantageous to belong to a rich and influential family; but, with a bit of good luck, anyone with talents could reach a high position, whatever his origin. Many generals, including some who became Emperors, rose from the ranks. Boys with intellectual gifts could enter the civil service and attain high office.[13] But the monasteries offered the best means for advancement. A bright novice would be noticed by the abbot and given special training. He might remain in the monastery and eventually become its abbot; or his reputation in monastic circles might be such that he would be offered a bishopric. He might be sent when young into a bishop's household, or even to the Patriarch's: where, if he did well, his career would be assured. Some of the Patriarchs were Imperial princes by birth; others were the sons of slaves.[14]

The Byzantine monasteries were so diverse and so mutually independent that it might have seemed impossible for them ever to combine to form a party. Indeed, during the earlier centuries of the Christian Empire they were not of great political importance, except in Egypt, where they had been longest established, but where they continually quarrelled amongst themselves. Occasionally a monastery that was well run and well connected, such as that of Sosthenion in Constantinople, could exercise pressure on a theological issue; but it operated through the hierarchy.[15] During these centuries it was the individual hermit or holy man who commanded the respect of the people. He might be itinerant, but more usually he settled himself in a permanent retreat, in a cave or on a rock or on a pillar. Soon all the pious folk of the district would come to see him, to consult him and to ask for his blessing. Even local governors would come to him for advice. The greatest of these hermits, Saint Symeon the Stylite, was so famous that Saint Genevieve of Paris, in faraway France, sent him a personal message of devotion, brought to him by a Syrian trader. The Emperors followed their subjects' example. When Saint Daniel the Stylite perched himself upon a column in Constantinople, Theodosius II felt such concern about him that whenever there was a rainstorm he would send to inquire how the saint had fared. Saint Alypius the Paphlagonian, who stood on a column for fifty-three years, till paralysis forced him to lie down, was elected abbot of a near-by monastery and governed it from his vantage-point. During the Iconoclastic persecution Saint Theodulus painted icons on his column-top, where the Emperor's police could not reach him. There were even two women Stylites.[16] But as time went on the individual hermit-saint began to disappear. This seems to have been due to a growing devotion to the Liturgy, which was enhanced by the victory of image-worship. The holy man who wished for solitude began to prefer to be near enough to some monastery, to which he could go to attend the Liturgy, and to which he therefore was attached. The last important hermit-saints lived in the tenth century. There was Luke the Stylite, whose column was at Chalcedon and who was consulted by members of the Lecapenus dynasty, as was his contemporary, Basil the Less. In the Greek peninsula there was Holy Luke of Styris, to whose cave men and women eagerly came for consultation.[17] Purely eremitical life was revived in the early fourteenth century by Gregory of Sinai, who thought participation in the Liturgy unnecessary for a mystic. But he found little support in Byzantine territory and moved to Bulgaria, from where his doctrines passed to Russia and eventually gave birth to that particularly Russian phenomenon, the *staretz*, or wandering hermit, of which the last and most notorious example was Grigor Rasputin.[18]

When a hermit-saint of importance died it was usual for a monastery to be erected on the spot, to carry on his holy influence. The great monastery of Saint Symeon Stylites near Aleppo had been an influential religious centre until the Arabs conquered the district. When Holy Luke of Styris died, the monastery church built over his hermitage was decorated by mosaicists sent from Constantinople by the Emperor.[19] Indeed, most monasteries had been founded to commemorate a saint or to house a holy relic. It was therefore natural that the monks should approve of the respect paid to holy pictures and holy relics. They were, too, in touch with the people and knew that such things gave reality to the Bible story and satisfied the popular need for a feeling of intimacy with the spiritual world. During the past few centuries it had been considered a supreme act of piety to found or endow a monastery. The numbers and the wealth of the monasteries had greatly increased. The Iconoclastic Emperors found in the monks their most dangerous opponents and took stern measures against them. Constantine V took a particular pleasure in closing their establishments and humiliating their persons. They were still too loosely organized to defend themselves effectively. But their sufferings brought them public sympathy; and Leo IV found it wise to modify his father's policy.[20] They played no active part in the restoration of image-worship under Irene, which was due to the determination and tact of the Empress and the layman, Tarasius, whom she had made Patriarch. But the monks by then had a spokesman in the abbot of Sakkudion in Bithynia, Platon: though his main contribution to the debates on the question of images was to oppose any show of tolerance to former Iconoclasts, however repentant they might be.[21] Platon's position, both as abbot of Sakkudion and as a spokesman for the monks, was inherited by his nephew Theodore, who moved in 799 to become abbot of the monastery of Studion, the greatest within the walls of Constantinople. Theodore was a great monastic reformer. His efforts to introduce a stricter discipline and more useful work into the monasteries were widely copied: though he failed in his attempt to establish a sort of Order in the Western sense, to which a chain of monasteries should belong. However, there were henceforward monks trained in the Studite tradition in all the greater monasteries, who kept in touch with each other and with Studion; their propaganda could reach monks all over the Empire. A definite monkish party can be said to have arisen.[22]

The party bore the stamp of Theodore's personality. The monks as a class resented any Imperial control of the Church. They could not prevent the Emperor from holding certain administrative rights. They did not deny him, for instance, the final decision in the appointment of the Patriarch. But they were determined that he should never dictate Church doctrine, as the Iconoclastic Emperors had done. He must obey the laws of the Church; he was not entitled from his position to be allowed any dispensation from them. But even more than they disliked an Emperor who meddled in doctrine or who broke a moral law they disliked a Patriarch who supported Imperial policy or who was ambitious for worldly power. In the Moechian dispute they continued to attack the Patriarch Tarasius for failing to excommunicate the priest who had performed the adulterous marriage service for Constantine VI long after Constantine was dead; and they never forgave Tarasius's successor, Nicephorus, for also withholding the excommunication that they demanded. Their protests against the Patriarch Methodius, when after the second restoration of image-worship he showed, as Tarasius had done, a readiness to let repentant Iconoclasts go unpunished, was in Theodore's tradition.[23] But after Theodore's death they abandoned some of his ideals. Theodore had a deep respect for learning. Half a century later the monkish party was definitely anti-intellectual. This was doubtless due to the encouragement given to learning by the Emperors of the second Iconoclastic period, especially Theophilus. The monks became suspicious of the Classical lore that flourished at the Court. They resented the Patriarch Methodius for not suppressing it, and, still more, Photius for delighting in it. There was a story that while Ignatius was Patriarch Photius invented a heresy for the amusement of seeing the monkish Patriarch flounder when he tried to discuss theology.[24] Somewhat later they abandoned another of Theodore's notions. He had urged the right of appeal to Rome, not that he believed in the supreme right of the Pope to pronounce on doctrine, but, of the Pentarchy of Patriarchs, whom he believed to be the final authority on matters of faith, the Pope was both the senior and the only one who could be trusted to give an independent and traditional answer. The Patriarch of Constantinople was too often the tool of the Emperor, while the Eastern Patriarchs all lived under infidel rule and could not afford to quarrel with the Emperor, who alone could use influence to protect them from the Caliph. But it was difficult to have the same faith in Rome when the Pope questioned the legality of the appointment of the Patriarch Ignatius, who was their leader; and Leo VI's appeal to Rome on the question of his fourth marriage and the Pope's condoning of what seemed to them sheer fornication, thoroughly blurred the issue. By the late tenth century monkish opinion in Constantinople was definitely hostile to Rome.[25]

Indeed, Leo VI's adroit handling of the *Tetragamia* affair weakened the monastic party and left it quiescent for half a century. When its leader, the saintly Euthymius, went over to the Emperor's side, and its former enemy, Nicholas Mysticus, became the champion of their moral cause, it was difficult for them to know what to think. When the fiery monk Polyeuct became Patriarch in 956, he seems to have won monastic support for all his many protests. But after his death the party once again quietened down, until Michael Cerularius won it to his side in his attack upon Rome. His propaganda, which enabled him successfully to defy the Emperor, was conducted mainly through the monks. But he lost their support when his worldly ambitions became too obvious.[26]

In the meantime the monks had been cowed partly by the formidable personality of the great warrior-Emperor, Basil II, and partly by the determination of the Emperors to reduce the material power of the monasteries. The military successes of the Empire had meant that all but the frontier provinces were freed from the dangers of enemy raids. It was therefore worth while to invest in land. The tenth century saw the growth of great secular estates, which, illegally but effectively, were absorbing numbers of free villages – that is to say, villages where land was held from the State in return for the duty of providing men for the Imperial army. But the villagers had also to pay heavy taxes. The local magnate, by offering to pay a good sum for the land or by offering to shoulder the tax-burden, could win control of the village; and the men went into his own private army. The monastic estates were not so dangerous politically. But on the lands that the monasteries acquired, usually by bequest, free villages similarly disappeared. The monks either cultivated the lands themselves, often inefficiently, or let them out to large tenant-farmers. Moreover, while, in theory at least, a layman's lands could be confiscated and re-allotted by the State, monastic lands were inalienable. In favour of the monasteries it should be remembered that, like the later Cistercians in the West, the monks often established themselves in bare and empty districts, such as the rocky promontory of Mount Athos, to which their labours brought prosperity. It should be remembered too that many of the monasteries were in cities and towns, without any landed endowments, though some might own a few neighbouring houses; and these urban monasteries did a vast amount of valuable social work, in providing hospitals, old people's homes and elementary schools. All the same, vast monastic estates acquired by bequest in prosperous parts of the country, often at a distance from the monasteries to which they belonged, were economically very unsatisfactory; and they were resented by the Imperial authorities, who were anyhow irritated by the political activities of the monks and their interference into the affairs of the hierarchy and even into those of the Imperial family.[27]

In 964 the Emperor Nicephorus II issued a law forbidding the creation of any new monastery or hospice or alms-house run by monks, and forbidding the gift or legacy of any further endowments to such institutions, except when an alms-house which was proved to be useful to the community was in danger of closing down. A second edict declared that all appointments to bishoprics should be subject to the Emperor's approval. He was anxious that the sees should not be filled by men of extreme monkish views. Nicephorus was known for his exemplary piety and his liking for the company of monks, and he had helped in the foundation of monasteries on Mount Athos. But, an ascetic himself, he disapproved of rich monasteries; and he was exasperated by the Patriarch Polyeuct.[28]

One of the conditions that Polyeuct imposed upon John Tzimisces before he would crown him was the repeal of Nicephorus's legislation as regards the monasteries.[29] It was a triumph for the monks. But their satisfaction was short-lived. Basil II devised a more practical way of humbling the monasteries. In 1003–4 he introduced a law which had the effect of imposing upon the local magnate the duty of paying all the taxes due from any village community in which he owned any property; and he applied it to the monasteries as well as to the lay landowners. It fell very heavily upon the monks, who depended mainly on their lands for their income. Many monasteries were forced to sell to the State large portions of their estates.[30]

Basil II's policy was abandoned by his successors. But the wealth of the monasteries had been reduced. Henceforward the monastic party was based on the monasteries in or near Constantinople, and its power lay in the influence that the monks could wield over the poorer people in the city. There had been a revival of spiritual and mystical monasticism at the end of the tenth century, under the guidance of the great teacher, Symeon, surnamed the New Theologian. This seems to have had some effect in guiding the country monasteries away from political interests.[31] But the monks of Constantinople were above all welfare officers, and they lived very much in the world. They maintained their tradition of resenting State interference in the Church, and criticizing the morals of the Court, with an increasing suspicion of the intellectual circles of the capital, and an increasing dislike of Rome, a dislike which Michael Cerularius used to such effect.[32]

The power of the monasteries in the countryside was further diminished by the troubles that befell the Empire in the latter decades of the eleventh century. The invasion of Asia Minor by the Seljuk Turks was disastrous for the monasteries there. Very few survived unharmed; and those that did lost touch with Constantinople. Not only did most of the monks in Cappadocia and the centre of the country flee from their establishments; even the monasteries on Bithynian Olympus, the most powerful centre of monastic activity in the old days, were driven out. Many monks fled to settle in the hills behind Trebizond, or near the Aegean coast, on Mount Latmos. But they were not secure there. Many more fled to the Greek islands or to the growing communities on

Mount Athos. Refugees always cause problems; and the European monasteries and the monasteries in the islands could not easily assimilate the influx. Few of them were rich. Even Mount Athos, which was to emerge as the leading monastic centre in centuries to come, was in a state of shocking disorder. The Emperor Alexius I had to send a commission there to inquire into reports of gross immorality amongst the monks. He ordered a strict tightening of their rules.[33]

Indeed, in the anxious years of the late eleventh century, when the Empire was facing invaders on every frontier, the monks could not afford to withhold co-operation with the government. But the monks of Constantinople were still ready to oppose immorality in high places. Alexius I Comnenus, soon after he had won the throne, tried, at his mother's prompting, to divorce his wife, Irene Ducaena, in order to marry the beautiful Dowager Empress, Maria of Alania. The Patriarch Cosmas refused to countenance the divorce, as he was a close friend of the Ducas family. But he knew he had monastic opinion behind him; for the two previous husbands of the Empress Maria were still alive. The general public, swayed by the monks, had been shocked at her marriage to the usurper Emperor Nicephorus Boteniates, when her husband, Michael VII Ducas, had been forced to become a monk. That she should repeat the offence and become a double adulteress was not to be tolerated. Alexius realized that he must abandon the scheme. Fortunately his marriage to Irene soon became a happy one and stood him in good stead, as Irene was deeply respected for her piety.[34]

In other matters Alexius was prepared to override the monks. When, in his desperate need for money, he confiscated gold and silver plate from the churches, there was no more than a mild protest from the hierarchy, and no objection from the monks, many of whom disapproved of ecclesiastical riches. They were less pleased when he began to make use of a system known as *charistikia*. By this system the estates of a monastery, even its town property, were given to a layman to administer. It was the business of the *charistikarios*, as he was called, to see that the monastery received all the money that it needed for its ordinary life and a sufficient reserve for emergencies, and he could keep the surplus revenue for himself. As a result, the land was more efficiently cultivated than before and the monks were not distracted by business affairs. It was, it seems, the Iconoclast who first devised the scheme; but when some bishops in the early eleventh century made use of it for monasteries under their charge, it was declared to be illegal. Alexius's uncle, Isaac Comnenus, seems to have been the first Emperor to donate *charistika* to friends and supporters; and his successors, with the exception of Constantine X Ducas, who disapproved of it, followed his example. Alexius made great use of the system. It enabled him to reward valuable servants at no cost to himself and at the same time to keep some control over monastic property. There were many ecclesiastics who welcomed the practice. The learned and saintly Eustathius of Thessalonica believed that it deterred the monks from thinking about money and enabled them to live more purely spiritual lives. Many of the more austere monks, especially in Constantinople, were not sorry to see their richer brethren forced into a less worldly way of life.[35]

However, the troubles of the Empire did not reduce the number of monks. The Jewish traveller Benjamin of Tudela, who visited Constantinople during the reign of Alexius's grandson, Manuel I, was told that there were as many churches in the city as there were days in the year.[36] The number is too neat to be true; but there were undoubtedly some two hundred churches, most of which were attached to some monastery or convent. Manuel certainly believed himself that there were too many monks in the city. In 1158 he issued an order that no new monastic establishment was henceforward to be founded in Constantinople or in any great city of the Empire. Furthermore, to secure the benefits of the *charistikia* system without its abuses, he ordered that new monastic foundations should not be endowed with land but with an income chargeable on the estate of the founder and his heirs, who thus became quite legitimately the *charistikarii*. Neither law was strictly obeyed, nor even remembered after Manuel's death.[37]

The monks had other problems during the twelfth century. They could make their opinion felt whenever the Emperor tried to improve relations with Rome, by giving support to any Patriarch who opposed him. But there were divisions amongst them, due to outbreaks of heresy. The Bogomil heresy spread from Bulgaria into Constantinople towards the end of the eleventh century, and there it met with other Dualist heresies, Messalian and Paulician, and a few minor sects, which had existed underground in the Empire and never been entirely suppressed. The Dualists, by insisting on the irredeemably evil nature of matter, could not accept the basic Christian doctrine of the Incarnation. The Church authorities could not condone them. The Dualists also offended the civil authorities by their social teachings. They were pacifists; they disapproved of the propagation of children; their attitude to the government and to the law was one of passive anarchism. But the emphasis that they laid on holy poverty attracted many of the more austere monks; and they acquired followers in a number of monasteries, including some of the richest and most renowned. Amongst the lay population they won respect through the severe and disciplined purity of their lives. But public opinion on the whole was embarrassed by their anti-social habits and shocked by their iconoclasm; for they disapproved not only of holy pictures and relics but also of holy symbols, some of them even rejecting the Cross as being a material object unworthy of reverence.[38] Some eminent lay folk were affected by the heresy, including, it seems, the Emperor Alexius I's mother, the former Regent Anna Dalassena, who was suddenly removed from the Court with a minimum of publicity.[39] Alexius himself took the lead in trying to stamp out the heresy, with measures that were sterner than many of the ecclesiastical leaders thought suitable.[40] He was not wholly successful. Heretic cells lasted on in some monasteries throughout the twelfth century. In 1147 the Emperor Manuel had the rare and not unenjoyable experience of being able to remove a Patriarch, Cosmas II, for harbouring heretics, winning the approval of the Church by so doing.[41]

With such internal problems to settle, neither the hierarchy nor the monasteries were in a position to challenge Imperial authority, except when they came together, with the backing of public opinion, to wreck Manuel's various attempts to be reconciled with the Church of Rome. Since the beginning of the century Byzantium had been feeling the effects of the Crusading movement, which, while at the outset it had been of some value to the Empire, had as time went on increased the mutual distrust and dislike between the Byzantines and the Westerners. To the ordinary Byzantine citizen it was horrifying to watch great armies from the West marching through his lands, apparently on the orders of the Pope, and pillaging as they went. He was shocked by the armed priests who marched with the armies. He was, furthermore, irritated by the number of Italian merchants who were settling in Constantinople and the other great cities of the Empire and dominating its commercial life. In the crises of the late eleventh century the Emperor had needed the help of the Italian maritime cities, and had paid for it by giving them trading concessions superior to those that his own subjects enjoyed. It was impossible for the people of Constantinople or of Thessalonica not to resent these haughty Westerners strutting through their streets and bazaars and enriching themselves at the expense of the local merchants; and when they brought their chaplains with them and were permitted to erect Latin churches, the anger increased. It is not surprising that Manuel's hope of reaching a better understanding with Rome – which, he thought, would be of political value – was frustrated by the refusal of Church and people alike to co-operate with him.[42]

Such opposition was, however, negative. Manuel, like his father, John II, and his grandfather, Alexius, kept a firm control over the Church in other matters. Apart from his Roman policy, his government was respected and obeyed. He himself lost no popularity when his taste for theology led him to advocate a doctrine, known as holosphyrism, which was to make

it easier for Muslims to accept Christianity, only to
see it dismissed as heresy by a Council which he
had summoned to discuss it. But the point was of
no great interest except to professional theologians.[43]
Even the monks thought it proper for an Emperor
to interest himself in such matters. Everyone was
far more shocked by an Emperor such as the usurper
Andronicus Comnenus, who begged his companions
not to discuss theology in his presence as he found it
so boring.[44] But Andronicus was a godless and blood-
thirsty man whose career did no credit to the throne;
and the monks played their part in bringing about
his fall. The Monkish party was still, and was to
remain, an essential factor in Byzantine life.

6

DECLINE AND FALL:
THE END OF THE KINGDOM
OF GOD ON EARTH

The twelfth century was the last period in which
Byzantium was still an Imperial power; and even
then its splendour was more apparent than real.
Constantinople was still the richest city in Christendom, with its factories and workshops and its busy
markets. But the money that was made there was
passing more and more into the purses of Italian
merchants. The Imperial army was still a formidable
fighting force; but it was composed mainly of foreign
mercenaries, costly to maintain and uncertain in their
loyalty. The social problems of the mid eleventh
century and the political problems that followed
upon the end of the Macedonian dynasty had combined with the irresponsible folly of the Emperors
and their advisers to allow Turkish invaders to sweep
over Anatolia and establish themselves in districts
that in the past had supplied most of the soldiers for
the army and most of the food for the capital. At the
same time upstart Normans attacked the Empire from
the West. The recovery under the first Comnenian
Emperors had been remarkable; but it was insecurely

based. It had been achieved largely through clever diplomacy, in particular by gaining the help of the Venetians, who demanded commercial privileges as their reward; and the other great Italian merchant-cities forcibly demanded similar advantages. The Crusading movement had been at first of use to the Empire; but almost from its outset it caused more ill will than goodwill between Eastern and Western Christendom; and the ill will increased as the schism between the Churches deepened.[1]

The Byzantines themselves sensed that they were living in a changing and uncertain world. Their feeling is visible in the art of the twelfth century. The art of the tenth and early eleventh centuries is a sure and serene art, classical in its proportions and its restraint but supra-human in its use of form and of light. It is an art that befits the kingdom of God on earth. In the twelfth century the sureness and serenity are shaken. Pathos comes in. There is an emotional exaggeration in proportions, and human anxieties and sorrows are revealed. Christ in majesty still dominates the domes of churches but He is a sterner God; and artists dwell, as never before, on Christ the suffering man. The Mother of God is no longer calm and proud. She is more often the *mater dolorosa*.[2] Indeed, the Empire could no longer feel complacent or secure. It had lost the Anatolian hinterland. Before the century was out, it no longer controlled the Balkan peninsula, where the Serbian and Bulgarian kingdoms had won their independence. It could no longer despise the countries of Western Christendom. It was increasingly aware that the West contained states with powerful armies and navies, and ambitious potentates who were unimpressed by Imperial Majesty.[3]

In these circumstances the strain of playing the role of a great power proved too much for Byzantium. In the last two decades of the twelfth century there was a rapid decline. Then early in the next century there came a sudden, dramatic and catastrophic crisis – in 1204, when an army of Crusaders, impelled by their own lawless greed and urged on by the calculated greed of the Venetians, took advantage of a peculiarly inept government in Constantinople to storm and sack the great city and to establish there a Latin Empire under a Frankish Emperor, with a Venetian viceroy to share his power.[4]

The conquerors failed to occupy the whole Empire. Byzantium survived in three parts. In the East a branch of the Comnenian dynasty set itself up in Trebizond. In the West a branch of the last dynasty, the Angeli, set itself up in Epirus. Nearer to the centre Theodore Lascaris, a son-in-law of the last Emperor, established a government in the ancient and holy city of Nicaea. Which of these was to be the official Empire-in-exile was not long in question. The Grand Comnenus in Trebizond, as he soon was to call himself, lived too far away. His Empire was to last until 1461; but it never played more than a peripheral part in the politics of Constantinople. The Angeli of Epirus were more formidable, especially after they captured the city of Thessalonica in 1223. But they were placed in a difficult geographical position; and they lacked the constitutional advantage enjoyed by Theodore Lascaris. This was the presence in his capital of the Patriarch of Constantinople.[5]

When Constantinople fell in 1204 the Patriarch, John X Camaterus, fled to Didymotichon in Thrace; but he did not formally abdicate, and he refused Theodore Lascaris's invitation to settle in Nicaea. Meanwhile the victorious Crusaders elected a Venetian, Thomas Morosini, to be Patriarch of Constantinople. He, with other Frankish and Italian bishops imposed upon Byzantine sees, tried to Latinize the Byzantine Church, forbidding Orthodox usages and the Orthodox Liturgy. On the news of John X's death in 1206 the Orthodox clergy living in the conquered territories came together and wrote to the Pope, Innocent III, to ask his permission to elect a Greek Patriarch who would acknowledge his authority but would conduct the Church along traditional Orthodox lines. Innocent had disapproved of the appointment of Morosini, but he was not prepared to disown him. The appeal of the Greeks received no answer. Had Innocent been statesman-like enough to listen to them and to have shown himself ready to protect the Orthodox against the intolerance of their new masters, he might have obtained recognition of his supremacy from the greater part of the Greek world. In their despair many Greeks would have accepted it; and it might have been difficult for the independent Greek princes to refuse to recognize a canonically elected Patriarch living in Constantinople. It might even have been possible for the Latin Emperor, Henry of Flanders – who did his best to befriend his Greek subjects and was liked by them, and who had probably inspired the letter to the Pope – to have been accepted by the Orthodox as a legitimate Emperor. But he could not influence the Pope: whose intransigence left the Orthodox world more bitter than before.[6]

So, when Theodore Lascaris sent out invitations to all the bishops of the Patriarchate to come to Nicaea to elect a Patriarch-in-exile, a number of bishops from the occupied territories arrived there to join the bishops from his own lands. But the rival Greek princes of Epirus and Trebizond forbade their clergy to attend. The Synod met in Nicaea in March 1208 and elected Michael Autorianus, who had been acting as head of the Church in Nicaean territory for the last three years. As soon as he was elected, Michael crowned Theodore Lascaris as Emperor.[7] The canonicity of the procedure was questionable. The Grand Comnenus and his Archbishop refused to recognize a Patriarch based on Nicaea until 1260. The Despot of Epirus, backed by the learned Archbishop of Ochrida, Demetrius Chomatianus, was even more

vehement in his condemnation. It was only when the
Nicaean Emperor recovered Constantinople in 1261
that the Patriarchal authority was admitted by all the
free Greek world. But the fact that the Nicaeans had
a Patriarch whom most of the Orthodox accepted
gave them an authority that neither of their rivals
possessed.[8]

In this era of crisis the Emperor and the Patriarch
had to work together. The Church could not afford
to quarrel with the lay authorities. Indeed, whatever
the monks might think, the official hierarchy had come
to accept the overriding rights of the Emperor. The
great canonist Theodore Balsamon, writing in about
1180, stated clearly that the Emperor was above the
law, both secular and religious, and that he alone
could introduce religious as well as secular legislation.
It was his business to care for the souls as well as
the bodies of his subjects. The only thing beyond his
power was to dictate on doctrine. Chomatianus, when
agitating for his master, Theodore Ducas Angelus,
to be recognized as Emperor and he himself, so he
hoped, as Patriarch, was even more explicit about
the rights of the lay ruler over the Church.[9]

The Empire of Nicaea under Theodore Lascaris
and his still abler son-in-law, John Vatatzes, was, in
spite of all its difficulties, a well-governed and prosperous state. By the time of John's death in 1254 it
was clear that it would be the Nicaeans who would
recover Constantinople from the Latins: whose pro-

longed hold of the capital was due far more to the rivalry of the Angeli with the Nicaeans than to their own efforts or to the help provided by the Venetians. In their government the Nicaean Emperors had the full co-operation of the hierarchy. It is true that the Patriarchs were not very happy with the Imperial policy of maintaining negotiations with Rome about the union of the Churches. But it was Roman intransigence rather than any sabotage by the Greeks that brought the talks to no result. The hierarchy was not particularly pleased when Theodore Lascaris married as his second wife the daughter of the Latin Emperor. But they only made an open protest when he planned to marry his own daughter to his new wife's brother, the Latin Emperor Robert. That would have been against the rules of consanguinity.[10] There were no objections when John Vatatzes married as his second wife Frederick II's bastard but legitimized daughter Constantia, as she joined the Orthodox Church, being rebaptized Anna.[11] The scholar-cleric Nicephorus Blemmydas boasted that he risked the Emperor's wrath by snubbing the the pretensions of her Italian lady-in-waiting, who was known to be the Imperial mistress.[12] But Blemmydas is not reliable on any matter concerning himself. He wanted desperately to become Patriarch, but in vain, as John Vatatzes and his son Theodore II after him were too wise to appoint so vain and cantankerous a man. Blemmydas would have us believe that Theodore II offered him the post, promising him, if he would accept it, more power and glory than any previous Patriarch had enjoyed, and that he accepted it, providing that he could always put first the glory of God. 'Never mind about the glory of God', said the Emperor crossly, and withdrew the offer. It is most unlikely that the offer was ever made.[13] Theodore II in his writings is perfectly explicit about the Emperor's complete authority over the Church: while Blemmydas, in the little tract on kingship that he dedicated to Theodore, declares that it is the Emperor's responsibility to see to the spiritual and moral welfare of his subjects.[14]

Nevertheless, the Emperor must himself obey the moral code. It was a shameless neglect of this principle that caused the next and last great quarrel between Church and State in Byzantium. Theodore II died in August 1268, leaving as his heir a son, John IV, who was aged eight. As the boy's mother was dead, Theodore had arranged that his chief minister, George Muzalon, should be regent, aided by the Patriarch, Arsenius Autoreanus. But Muzalon, a bureaucrat of humble birth, was despised by the army and by the nobles of the Court: while the Patriarch, though a layman until his election, proved to be an ascetic disciplinarian, much admired by the monks and the poorer clergy, but disliked by his bishops. Within a few days Muzalon was murdered; and the leading general in the Empire, Michael Palaeologus, a distant cousin of the Emperor's, was installed as Megas Dux and regent, and took, with the Patriarch's consent, the title of Despot. Then, in December, he demanded that the Patriarch should crown him Emperor. Arsenius seems to have agreed grudgingly that this was the best solution. There had been precedents in the tenth century of soldiers taking over the autocracy when the lawful Emperor was a minor, without prejudice to the ultimate rights of the lawful Emperor. But neither Nicephorus Phocas nor John Tzimisces had had sons, whereas Michael had a large family. So Arsenius insisted that the boy John should be crowned by him at the same time. But at the ceremony Michael pushed himself ahead of the boy, so as to be crowned first, as befitted the man who was to be autocrat. Arsenius had to content himself by obliging Michael to take a solemn oath that he would do nothing against the interests or the person of his colleague.[15]

Michael's reign began gloriously. In 1259 his troops won a great victory at Pelagonia, in Thessaly, over a coalition of Frankish princes, the King of Sicily and the Despot of Epirus. The power of the Angeli was broken; and Michael obtained from the Franks a foothold in the Peloponnese, which his successors would steadily enlarge. Two years later, in July 1261, his army entered Constantinople; and the Latin Empire was ended.[16] There was rejoicing throughout the Empire. Even Arsenius, who had retired from the Patriarchate because of his suspicions of Michael, agreed to return to his throne and to perform a new coronation ceremony in Saint Sophia. But, whatever the Patriarch might have expected, the young Emperor John was not present. It was Michael, his wife, and his eldest son who were crowned. Before the end of the year Arsenius discovered that Michael had put out John's eyes, so as to disqualify him for ever from sitting on the throne. This was too much. Arsenius excommunicated Michael and forbade him to enter the Church of Saint Sophia.[17]

Opinion in the Empire was divided. The Emperor Michael had performed a monstrous act of cruelty against a child who had been committed to his care, and in so doing he had broken a solemn oath. Pious folk could not fail to be horrified. The resentment was especially strong in the Asiatic provinces, where the old dynasty was remembered with affection. Indeed, there were two abortive risings there in the name of the blind and imprisoned young Emperor. On the other hand, Michael was the crowned Emperor. Could a Patriarch excommunicate the Emperor? Even Nicholas Mysticus had not ventured to excommunicate Leo VI for tricking him over his fourth marriage, though he had gone so far as to shut the doors of Saint Sophia in the Emperor's face. Moreover, however great his sin, Michael had shown himself to be a gloriously successful Emperor, whose efforts had clearly been blessed by God; and no one in Constantinople nor in the European provinces had ever seen the young victim, whose existence had hardly been noticed. Feeling ran high. On the one side there was the monkish party, led now by the Patriarch himself, a party that had always demanded a high standard of morality which even the Emperor should respect and that had never been hesitant in reproving the lax and luxurious habits of the Court and the easy-going intellectuals who now filled so many of the bishops' sees. On the other side there was the Court party, which was less pious and strict but no less religious, holding that the Emperor was the Viceroy of God, and a Viceroy who had done great things for God's Church. He had sinned, maybe; but as Emperor he must be given a dispensation. To the monks it was intolerable that a sinful man, whatever his rank, should regard himself as being above the laws of God. To the Court the monks seemed to be disowning the basic and holy constitution of the Christian Empire.[18]

The rift was to last for many years. It was not till 1265 that Michael ventured to depose Arsenius, on the grounds of his complicity in a plot against the throne. The evidence was almost certainly faked, as Arsenius, much as he hated Michael, was not a political conspirator. The Patriarch whom the Emperor then installed, Germanus III, was a foolish man, utterly lacking in dignity. He was of no help to the Emperor, who forced him to abdicate. Late in 1266 Michael appointed in his stead a monk, Joseph, who, after few months of earnest debate, agreed to absolve him of his sin. On 2 February 1267, the Emperor knelt bare-headed in front of the Patriarch and the Holy Synod and confessed his sin. The ban of the Church was then lifted from him.[19]

It was a triumph for the Church as the guardian of morality. The Emperor had been forced to admit that he had sinned as a man. But it did not end the schism. Arsenius, living miserably in exile, pronounced himself to be satisfied. But the Arsenites, as his followers were called, were less indulgent. Many of the bishops, supported by the Patriarch of Alexandria, who preferred to live in comfort in Constantinople rather than under Muslim rule in Egypt, refused to recognize Joseph as Patriarch. Large numbers of monks followed their example. The monasteries were ordered to eject such rebels, with the result that they wandered homeless round the Empire, winning sympathy for their cause. Some of them preached non-co-operation not only with the Patriarchate but also with the lay government. They created considerable embarrassment for the authorities, especially as they were supported by neighbours who were jealous of Michael, such as John the Bastard, a prince of the Angelus family who had made himself ruler of Thessaly. He held a Synod in their support in 1272.[20]

The Emperor did not improve his relations with the monks by his external policy. There was a very real danger that the Latin West would make a powerful attempt to re-capture Constantinople, under the forceful leadership of Charles of Anjou, King of Sicily. Michael came to believe that the only way to counter this was by negotiating the union of his Church with Rome. It was not an easy policy. Many Popes preferred that the Greek Church should have to submit through conquest. But when Pope Gregory X, a man devoted to the idea of the Crusade, ascended the throne in 1271, Rome took a more conciliatory line, while still insisting on recognition of her supremacy. In 1274 Michael was invited to send delegates to the Council of Lyons, to offer the submission of his Church.

His acceptance of the invitation was far from popular in Byzantium. There were a few clerics, such as John Beccus, Grand Chartophylax of Saint Sophia, who became genuinely convinced that the Roman case was valid. But on the whole it was only amongst the laymen of the Court that any supporters of union could be found; and they were moved by political rather than religious considerations. The Patriarch Joseph disapproved. He did not abdicate, but he was temporarily suspended. The only clerics whom the Emperor found willing to go to Lyons were the discredited ex-Patriarch, Germanus, and the Metropolitan of Nicaea, Theophanes, who was far from enthusiastic. It was the Emperor's lay Secretary, George Acropolita, who acted as spokesman for the party. The delegation sailed in two ships; and the

pious were not surprised to learn that they ran into
a fierce storm, in the course of which the ship con-
taining the gifts destined for the Pope was lost with
all its contents.[21]

The Union of Lyons was signed in July 1274.
Politically, it achieved its immediate object for
Michael. Charles of Anjou was restrained from attacking Constantinople for the time being. But the threat
remained, and was not entirely removed till 1282,
when, as the outcome of a plot largely organized at
Constantinople, Charles's troops in Italy were slaugh-
tered in the uprising known as the Sicilian Vespers.
In the meantime there was bitter controversy in
Byzantium. The great majority of the bishops, led
by the Patriarch Joseph, opposed the Union. Joseph
was deposed in 1275 and replaced by the Unionist,
John Beccus; but Michael could not afford to depose
other bishops, for the lack of candidates willing to
accept his policy. Several of the bishops felt that
Joseph had not been forceful enough in denouncing
the Union, and left him to join the Arsenites – who
were not sorry to have another weapon with which
to attack the government, knowing that they would
have popular support. In lay circles, too, the Union
was generally detested; and the opposition was led
by the Emperor's own sister, Eulogia. For the first
time since the Iconoclasts an Emperor imprisoned
and even tortured pious Christians for refusing to
obey his religious dictation. When Michael died in

December 1282, he was hated by the greater part of his subjects for having signed the Union and having tried to force it on them, and excommunicated by the Pope for having failed to make them accept it.[22]

His son and successor, Andronicus II, reigned for thirty-nine years, until 1321. It was a disastrous period politically for Byzantium, during which almost all its Asiatic territory was lost to the young Ottoman Turkish emirate and much of the European lands lost to the Serbs, and there were recurrent economic problems and political unrest. Religiously it was important as it set the pattern for the relations between Church and State for the remaining years of the Empire. Andronicus was a pious man. As a boy he had been made by his father to subscribe to the Union; but he was unhappy about it. Though he was personally fond of the Unionist Patriarch, John Beccus, he at once deposed him and re-instated Joseph. He released all the victims of Michael's persecution. In January 1283 a synod which he summoned ordered the burning of all the documents connected with the Union. Beccus was convicted of heresy and exiled, but not ill-treated.[23]

The Patriarch Joseph died soon afterwards, in March. The new Emperor was already in touch with the leaders of the Arsenites, who hoped that one of their number might be appointed to succeed Joseph and were disappointed when the Emperor chose instead the scholar George of Cyprus, who became

Gregory II. Another synod was held at once to complete the condemnation of the Unionists, including the late Emperor himself. Most of the Orthodox were now satisfied; but the extreme Arsenites remained implacable. Andronicus personally interviewed their spokesmen. He brought the body of Arsenius to Constantinople and re-buried it with full Patriarchal honours; and he even went to visit the blind ex-Emperor, John Lascaris. But the Arsenites still refused to co-operate with him.[24]

Gregory II was deposed in 1289 for issuing a *tomos* which, he hoped, would reconcile the Unionists but which both Latins and Greeks considered heretical. His successor was a monk from Mount Athos, which was now becoming the chief centre for monastic thought. Athanasius I was a virtuous man with an active social conscience, but he was a harsh and tactless disciplinarian, whom it was difficult to like. After four years he was so unpopular that the Emperor replaced him by a more genial monk, John XII. But John too developed a social conscience. He threatened to resign in 1299, in protest against the marriage of the Emperor's five-year-old daughter, Simonis, to the middle-aged and dissolute King of Serbia; and after he had been persuaded to stay, he began to criticize the government's fiscal policy, taking it upon himself to act, as Athanasius had done, as the champion of the poor. Andronicus removed him in 1303 and recalled Athanasius. But Athanasius was just as high-minded and still more high-handed than before and interfered more and more in social politics. In 1309 he was at last induced to resign, to the relief not only of the Emperor but also of all the bishops. Meanwhile the poor had not been particularly grateful either to him or to John XII for their championship; and the Arsenites detested them both. It was not the Patriarch's business to meddle in politics. As it has been said, Athanasius treated the Empire as though it were his monastery.[25]

The Emperor's next choice, Niphon, Bishop of Cyzicus, was of a very different stamp, being a worldly and not over-scrupulous man who was known to be a tactful administrator. He showed his ability by achieving almost immediately a reconciliation with the Arsenites. An encyclical that he issued in September 1310 celebrated their return to the Church. The terms of the settlement were drawn up by the Emperor's minister, Nicephorus Choumnus, and set forth in an Imperial chrysobull. The Arsenites agreed to recognize the Patriarch and the hierarchy. But they insisted that the name of the Patriarch Joseph should be erased from the list of Patriarchs. The document ordering the erasure declared that so holy a man would not have wished to be commemorated for a worldly office. A few extremists rejected the settlement and remained in revolt against the hierarchy. But these Religious Zealots, as they were called, had little influence.[26]

Andronicus was helped by his reputation for piety. This enabled him to keep control of the Church. The Patriarch Niphon was dismissed in 1314 for simony. Andronicus waited a year before making his next appointment. The new Patriarch, John XIII Glycas, was a quiet but capable scholar, who retired because of ill health in 1319. After a few months an elderly monk, Gerasimus I, was appointed; but he died in 1321. The post was then left vacant for two years. It was then given to another monk, Esaias. After his experience with Athanasius and John XII, Andronicus was not unhappy to do without a Patriarch. Besides, it enabled him to proceed more smoothly with the re-organization of the Church.[27]

There was need for re-organization. The rapid loss of territory, particularly to the infidel Turks, and resulting movements of population made the old episcopal boundaries out-of-date. Some cities had fallen irrevocably into enemy hands. Others had been deserted owing to enemy raids. Others were practically isolated. At first Andronicus seems, rather surprisingly, to have added to the number of bishops, probably because he was anxious that isolated communities should not be deprived of spiritual pastors. Eventually the numbers were reduced and the pattern made more realistic. It was essential to have an efficient episcopate. As the enemy advanced lay Imperial officials necessarily withdrew. It was the bishop who remained to look after the Christian population. It was he who had to negotiate with the conquerors for the welfare of his flock. It was he who tried to preserve church buildings and church endowments, and who was considered responsible by the new masters for the good behaviour of the Christians and their payment of taxes. He became, so to speak, the representative of the Emperor *in partibus infidelium.* It was therefore important for the Emperor to control episcopal appointments and to see that the bishops did not desert their sees when they were overrun by the infidel.[28] At the same time Andronicus was ready to add to the privileges of the Patriarchate, giving it control of the monasteries that had hitherto depended directly upon the Emperor, including the great monastic republic of Mount Athos.[29]

Andronicus II governed the Church well enough, but as a lay ruler he was far from successful. It was typical of him that when at a meeting of his ministers one of them fell into a mystic trance he was impressed and edified.[30] As he and his advisers grew older the administration became more and more incompetent. Andronicus himself began to revive his father's policy of negotiation with Rome, which lost him popularity.[31] About the same time he announced an increase in taxation, which was bitterly resented. His family life was unhappy. His eldest son, the co-Emperor Michael, died in 1320, leaving a son, Andronicus, who had been crowned co-Emperor in 1316, but who had recently caused the death of his own brother in an

unseemly brawl. The old Emperor decided to dis-
inherit him. This was too much for Andronicus III,
who, encouraged by the younger members of the
Court and the aristocracy, rose in revolt in 1321. The
civil war lasted on and off for seven years. Public
opinion was generally on the side of the young
Emperor; and in 1327 the Patriarch Esaias was
imprisoned by Andronicus II for refusing to excommunicate him. Had the young man's party not been
hampered by jealousies and intrigues, he would have
triumphed far sooner. As it was, it was only in 1328
that he gained complete control of Constantinople
and forced his grandfather to abdicate.[32]

Despite his unsavoury past and the appalling circumstances of the Empire that he had inherited,
Andronicus III showed talent as a ruler. He was
greatly aided by his chief minister and close friend,
John Cantacuzenus. Unfortunately, he died in 1341,
leaving as his heir a child of six, John V. Cantacuzenus
expected to be given the regency, as the boy's mother,
Anna of Savoy, had neither the ability nor the will to
carry on the government. But he was opposed by
two men who had owed their careers to him; a rich
noble, the Admiral Alexius Apocaucus, and the
Patriarch John Calecas. John XIV was the last
Patriarch of the Empire to have political ambitions.
He had twice acted as governor of Constantinople
when Andronicus III had been campaigning, and he
considered himself well qualified to govern the

Empire. He had, moreover, the confidence of the Empress-Mother. But the position of a Patriarch-Regent was never secure; so he called in the help of Apocaucus, who was bitterly jealous of Cantacuzenus. Late in 1341, when Cantacuzenus was away on a campaign, he was stripped of his offices; and, with the consent of the Empress, the Patriarch and Apocaucus took over the government. The outcome was six years of devastating civil war. Cantacuzenus had the support of the countryside in general, which followed the lead of the local nobility. A scholar himself, he had the sympathy of the intellectuals. But he was disliked in the towns throughout the Empire as a representative of the nobility, and particularly in Constantinople, where, as usual, there was a sentimental loyalty to the legitimate dynasty. The Church was divided. The Patriarch had most of the higher clergy on his side, and at first, it seems, the monks in the cities. The provincial clergy and monasteries supported Cantacuzenus.[33] But the alignment was complicated by a contemporaneous and very bitter religious controversy, the so-called Hesychast controversy, which dealt with the theory of mysticism. The Hesychast doctrine, put forward by the monk Gregory Palamas, was that the true mystic could in the end see God, not in His essence but in His energies, that is to say, His uncreated light. The doctrine was challenged by a Calabrian-born scholar, Barlaam, who made fun of the Hesychasts on the ground that they recommended as an exercise in concentration that one should stare at one's navel. Cantacuzenus supported Palamas, but Apocaucus was not unsympathetic towards him, nor was the Empress. The Patriarch John Calecas bitterly opposed the doctrine, and had on his side many of the nobility, headed by Irene Choumna, the daughter of the great minister Nicephorus Choumnus and the widow of one of Andronicus II's sons. Of Cantacuzenus's scholarly friends, Nicephorus Gregoras, who was strongly anti-Roman, and Demetrius Cydones, who became a convert to Rome, both disliked the doctrine, while the lay mystic, Nicholas Cabasilas, after some hesitation, came down in its favour. Palamas himself had friendly feelings towards Rome; but the Papal Legate, Paul of Smyrna, denounced Palamism as heresy. It was left to the government of the time to summon Councils which should approve or condemn it, the members voting as the authorities directed. A Council in June 1341 over which Andronicus III presided, and a Council held two months later under the presidency of Cantacuzenus as regent, both gave approval to Palamism, but a Synod in 1344, summoned by the Patriarch with the grudging consent of the Empress, denounced Palamas as a heretic and ordered his imprisonment. The Empress, after quarrelling with the Patriarch, arranged for a Synod in February 1347, which reversed this decision; and later that year, when Cantacuzenus had at last ended the civil war

by entering Constantinople, a Council which he summoned as Emperor – and which was attended by
representatives of the other Orthodox Churches and
was therefore in Orthodox eyes Oecumenical – ac-
claimed the doctrine of the Energies of God as being
truly Orthodox. The story showed that, even in a
dispute so intense that it divided families and broke
old friendships, and one that was purely concerned
with theology, Church Councils would obey the
dictation of the representatives of Imperial authority:
though it is fair to say that the final outcome corres-
ponded with the views of the greater part of the
Church.[34]

There was a similar lack of logic in the strange
movement of the Political Zealots of Thessalonica, a
group of poorer citizens who seized power there in
1342 and held it for seven years, at first in nominal
loyalty to the legitimate Emperor, John V, but later
in defiance of all Imperial authority. The Zealots
despoiled the local nobility and the rich merchants
of the city, slaughtering many of them, and confiscated
the property of the monasteries; and they regarded
Cantacuzenus as their chief enemy and would not
allow Palamas to enter the city when he was appointed its Archbishop. Yet they showed favours to
the poorer clergy and monks, who elsewhere were
the political supporters of Cantacuzenus and the
religious supporters of Palamas. When at last they
fell, it was not any government official but Palamas

who, by his benevolence and charity and his refusal to countenance reprisals, restored concord to the city.[35]

Though the Imperial control of the Church was recognized, there were still limits beyond which a wise Emperor would not go. John V, who reigned nominally for fifty years but was at times subordinated to his father-in-law, John VI Cantacuzenus, his son, Andronicus IV, and his grandson, John VII, was himself convinced of the need for friendship with the West, even if it meant Church-union with Rome. When visiting Italy in 1369 he made his personal submission to the Pope; but he would not commit his subjects, though he promised to do his best to convert them.[36] His tact was rewarded. Towards the end of his reign a document was issued which definitely laid down the Emperor's rights over the Church. There were nine points. The Emperor was to nominate metropolitans by making his choice from three candidates submitted to him; he alone could redistribute sees; appointments to high administrative offices in the Church had to have his approval; neither he nor his senior officials could be excommunicated without his sanction; every bishop must take an oath of allegiance to him on appointment; bishops must obey his orders about coming to Constantinople and returning to their sees; every bishop must sign acts passed by a Synod or Council; every bishop must implement such acts and refuse support to any cleric or candidate for ecclesiastical office who opposed such acts or Imperial policy in general.[37]

The territory of the Patriarchate was by now far larger than that of the shrunken Empire. But by controlling the episcopate the Emperor could keep some control over the Orthodox world. He was still the Holy Emperor, God's viceroy on earth, as the Patriarch Antony IV sharply reminded the Grand Prince of Muscovy, Basil I, who was proposing to omit the Emperor's name from the liturgy. The Emperor was still, Antony wrote, the consecrated head of the Oecumene, the King whom Saint Peter bade the faithful to honour. As Antony saw it, the Eusebian conception still endured.[38]

John V's son, Manuel II, tested the concordat when in about 1414 he transferred a Macedonian bishop to the see of Moldavia. The Patriarch protested, nominally on the grounds that a bishop could not be transferred but actually, it seems, because the Emperor had no control over Moldavia, and the Patriarch feared that the Prince of Moldavia might take offence. Manuel won his point.[39]

It was tested again when Manuel's son, John VIII, determined to take a delegation to Italy in order to unite his Church with the Roman. Manuel at the end of his life had advised John to maintain negotiations with Rome but never to commit himself, as there never could be real union.[40] But John was desperate. The Empire could not survive without help from the West. He used his authority to drag a company of bishops and learned laymen with him to the Union Congress which was opened at Ferrara in 1438 and soon transferred to Florence. There the Greeks, individualists dragooned by the Emperor, were no match for the well-trained and well-ordered team of Latin divines. Some of the Greeks were genuinely convinced by the Roman argument, others by the political necessity; others could not disobey the Emperor, who put pressure on them all to sign the act of Union. Only one bishop defied him, Mark Eugenicus, Metropolitan of Ephesus, who was later relieved of his see.[41] But John discovered, as so many Emperors had discovered before him, the limitations of Imperial power. When he returned to Constantinople he found public opinion so passionately opposed to the Union that not only was it impossible for him to implement it, but many of the bishops who had been known to favour it were shunned by their congregations and migrated to Italy.[42] It was only in the winter of 1452, when the Sultan's armies were gathering for the final assault on the Christian capital, that John's brother, Constantine XI, was able at last to have the Union formally proclaimed in Saint Sophia, by a Cardinal who had brought with him a handful of troops to encourage the desperate citizens. Even so, though no one challenged the authority of the Emperor, the faithful began to avoid Saint Sophia and any other church that was served by Unionist clergy. Only on the very last evening of the siege, when it was known that the morrow would be the fateful day, all who could do so came to join the Emperor for a final liturgy in Saint Sophia, forgetting all discord at last. It was too late. On 29 May 1453 the Christian Empire, the Kingdom of God on earth, came to an irrevocable end.[43]

To the last the Eusebian theory had endured, coloured in varied tints down the centuries but structurally unaltered. Eusebius would have approved of the words of the Patriarch Antony, written over a thousand years after his death. Byzantium has often been misrepresented as a static society. It was not static. Its arts and its sciences progressed, though the pace was sometimes slow. It adapted its administration from time to time, to suit changing circumstances. But it was conservative in the truest sense of the word. The Byzantines believed that it was their duty and their privilege to conserve the great cultures of the past, of Greece and of Rome, whose heirs they were, imbued with the Christian spirit, in order that civilization itself might endure in a dark and uncertain world. Their religious sense was sincere and intense. They were deeply conscious of eternity, and deeply conscious, too, that the divine is beyond human understanding and can only be interpreted through symbols. The earthly Empire was an ephemeral thing. It could only be justified if it were brought into relation with the Kingdom of Heaven.

The Kingdom of Heaven was the unseen, everlasting Idea. The kingdom on earth could not be more than its earthly shadow, a tangible but transient symbol that should be a preparation for eternity. To fulfil its role it must be righteous and harmonious, and dominated by the True Faith, as far as the True Faith could be known. But sin stalks through the temporal world. The Byzantines were well aware that their history was full of tales of frailty and folly, of pride, ambition and greed. It was their sinfulness, they believed, that caused their decline and fall. But the ideal remained high, however far its practical realization might fall short of the ideal. It was a genuine attempt to set up a Christian commonwealth on earth that would be in harmony with Heaven.

In fact the origins of the conception were pagan. It was Platonic thought, transmitted by such interpreters as the pagan Plotinus, the Jew Philo, and the Christian heretic Origen, which was combined with the Oriental tradition of Hellenistic monarchy and the pragmatic authority of the Roman Imperator, that formed the foundation on which Eusebius built up his theory of government. But the theory endured because the Byzantines, for all their piety, were practical. They knew that the Emperor, whatever he might symbolize, was a mere man. In spite of the coronation ceremony, he was not a priest. Indeed, as it was his business to lead armies into battle and sit in judgment in secular courts, he could not be a priest. His divine monarchy was limited. He must not pronounce on doctrine; the defeat of Iconoclasm made that clear. Doctrine was a matter only for a Council of all the bishops within the oecumene, on whom the Holy Spirit would descend as It descended on the disciples at Pentecost. Though he was above the Law, yet he must respect it as the guarantor of harmony. Leo VI had broken his own law, by his fourth marriage; and though he was given a dispensation, the *tomus* that closed the controversy indicated that he had done wrong. He must not commit crimes against morality. Michael VIII had to do penance for his treatment of John IV. If his crimes were intolerable, the people would rise and drag him from the throne, as they dragged Phocas and Andronicus I. It he were dangerously incompetent the army or the Palace officials would see to his disposal. The man must be worthy of his job; but if he were, then he was unquestionably the Autocrat.

Despite the efforts of men like Photius and Michael Cerularius, the Patriarch was unquestionably his subordinate. Public opinion approved of the Patriarch acting as the keeper of the Empire's, and the Emperor's, conscience; but he must not put himself on a level with the Emperor, nor meddle in lay politics. After all, God in Heaven has no High Priest there to limit His power. God's viceroy on earth should be similarly unhampered. There was, however, always a vocal minority in Byzantium which challenged the right of the Emperor to give orders to the Church and which, when organized by monastic leaders such as Theodore the Studite, could embarrass and sometimes influence Imperial policy. But, for all its activities, it never succeeded in breaking down the Eusebian constitution.

No form of government can survive for very long without the general approval of the public. In spite of the monks, the ordinary man and woman in Byzantium believed their Empire to be God's holy empire on earth, with the holy Emperor as representative of God before the people and the representative of the people before God. For eleven centuries, from the days of the first Constantine to those of the eleventh, the theocratic constitution of the Christian Roman Empire was essentially unchanged. No other constitution in all the history of the Christian era has endured for so long.

NOTES

CHAPTER I   THE CHRISTIAN EMPIRE

1 Eusebius of Caesarea, *Vita Constantini*, ed. I. A. Heikel, *Griechische Christliche Schriftsteller*, VI–VII, *Eusebius Werke* (Leipzig, 1902), I, pp. 21 ff. Eusebius, writing in Greek, gives the words that Constantine saw as being in Greek. He does not tell us whether Constantine in fact saw them in Latin.

2 Lactantius, *De Mortibus Persecutorum*, ed. J. Moreau (Paris, 1954), p. 44 and notes, pp. 436–42.

3 See N. H. Baynes, 'Constantine the Great and the Christian Church', *Proceedings of the British Academy*, XV (1929), pp. 9–10, 60–5.

4 *Ibid. passim*; F. Dvornik, *Early Christian and Byzantine Political Philosophy* (Dumbarton Oaks Studies, Washington, 1966), II, pp. 634–5.

5 For a good summary of the ecclesiastical organization see A. H. M. Jones, *Constantine and the Conversion of Europe* (London, 1948), pp. 45–6.

6 See E. Amann, 'Novatianisme', *Dictionnaire de Théologie Catholique*, ed. Vacant, Mangenot and Amann, XI, i (1931), coll. 816–49.

7 See H. I. Bell, *Jews and Christians in Egypt* (London, 1924), pp. 38–99; Amann, 'Mélitiens', *Dictionnaire de Théologie Catholique*, X, i (1928), coll. 531–6.

8 W. H. C. Frend, *The Donatist Church* (Oxford, 1952), esp. pp. 141 ff.; Jones, *Constantine*, pp. 103–7.

9 Baynes, 'Constantine the Great', pp. 10–12; Frend, *Donatist Church*, pp. 150 ff.

10 Baynes, 'Constantine the Great', 12–13, giving texts, and pp. 75–8.

11 *Ibid.* pp. 13–14, 75–8.

12 *Ibid.* pp. 14–16; Jones, *Constantine*, pp. 107–9; Frend, *Donatist Church*, pp. 155–9.

13 See H. M. Gwatkin, *Studies of Arianism* (Cambridge, 1900), pp. 14–42; X. Le Bachelet, 'Arianisme', *Dictionnaire de Théologie Catholique*, I, ii, coll. 1779 ff.

14 Eusebius, *Vita Constantini*, II, pp. 67–71.

15 Jones, *Constantine*, pp. 149–51; Baynes, 'Constantine the Great', pp. 20–1, 84–5.

16 See E. Honigmann, 'Recherches sur les listes des Pères de Nicée et de Constantinople', *Byzantion*, XI (Brussels, 1936), esp. pp. 429–39.

17 Baynes, 'Constantine the Great', pp. 87–90.

18 C. J. Hefele, *Histoire des Conciles*, ed. and trans. by H. Leclercq (Paris, 1907–52), cited henceforward as Hefele–Leclercq, I, i, pp. 436–42; Jones, *Constantine*, pp. 159–60, giving a summary of the Creed of Caesarea.

19 Hefele–Leclercq, pp. 434–5, 442. See Jones, *Constantine*, pp. 161–3. Hefele, relying on Athanasius, who was not unprejudiced, rather than on Eusebius, plays down the part of the Emperor. See also A. E. Burn, *The Council of Nicaea* (London, 1925), pp. 29 ff., esp. 36–7.

20 See Jones, *Constantine*, p. 163.

21 Hefele–Leclercq, pp. 488–503; Bell, *Jews and Christians*, pp. 40–1. As Bell shows, the Melitian Church did not entirely disappear but lasted on for about another century.

22 Baynes, 'Constantine the Great', p. 21; Jones, *Constantine*, p. 172.

23 Baynes, 'Constantine the Great', pp. 22–3; Jones, *Constantine*, pp. 172–80.

24 Baynes, 'Alexandria and Constantinople: a Study in Ecclesiastical Diplomacy', in Baynes, *Byzantine Studies and other Essays* (London, 1955), pp. 102 ff.; Bell, *Jews and Christians*, pp. 45–71.

25 Eusebius, *Vita Constantini*, II, p. 126. See Baynes, 'Constantine the Great', pp. 25–6, 90–1.

26 Baynes, 'Constantine the Great', pp. 26–7: Jones, *Constantine*, pp. 207–8.

27 Athenagoras, *Supplicatio pro Christianis*, in *Corpus Apologetarum Christianorum Saeculi Secundi*, ed. J. T. Otto, VI (Jena, 1857), p. 184.

28 Tertullian, *Liber ad Scapulam*, in J. P. Migne, *Patrologia Latina*, I, col. 778.

29 Dvornik, *Early Christian and Byzantine Philosophy*, II, pp. 280–1. For a full discussion of the subject and an ample bibliography see K. H. Bernhardt, *Das Problem der altorientalischen Königsideologie im Alten Testament* (Leiden, 1961).

30 Dvornik, *Early Christian and Byzantine Philosophy*, I, pp. 84–101.

31 *Ibid.* vol. I, pp. 9–19.

32 Aristotle, *Politics*, ed. H. Rackham (Loeb edn, London, 1932), p. 246; Isocrates, *Address to Philip* (Loeb edn, London, 1928), pp. 322 ff.

33 Joannes Stobaeus, *Anthologium*, ed. C. Wachsmuth and O. Hense, IV (Berlin, 1909), pp. 82 ff., 265, 270, 278. See Baynes, 'Eusebius and the Christian Empire', in Baynes, *Byzantine Studies*, pp. 168–72, where the relation between Eusebius and the philosophers quoted by Stobaeus is shown; see also Dvornik, *Early Christian and Byzantine Philosophy*, I, pp. 245–69.

34 Plutarch, *Moralia: To an Uneducated Ruler*, ed. H. N. Fowler (Loeb edn, London, 1936), pp. 52–70.

35 Philo, *Legatio ad Gaium*, ed. F. H. Colson (Loeb edn, London, 1962), pp. 76–82; Origen, *Contra Celsum*, ed. P. Koetschau, in *Die griechischen christlichen Schriftsteller der ersten drei Jahrhunderte*, II (Leipzig, 1899), p. 158.

36 Eusebius, *De Laudibus Constantini*, ed. Heikel, II, p. 201.

37 See Baynes, 'Constantine the Great', pp. 95–103, for a general account of Constantine's views and aims.

CHAPTER 2   THE VICEROY OF GOD

1 For the history of Constantine's sons see E. Stein, *Histoire du Bas-Empire* (Brussels, 1959), I, pp. 131–57.

2 See G. Bardy, 'La Réaction Eusébienne et le Schisme de Sardique', in A. Fliche and V. Martin, *Histoire de l'Église*, III (Paris, 1939), pp. 113–30.

3 Quoted by Athanasius, *Historia Arianorum*, in Migne, *Patrologia Graeco-Latina*, XXV, col. 748.

4 Athanasius, *Historia Arianorum*, coll. 728, 733, 749, 773, 776. It should be noted that Gregory of Nazianzus, a kinder and wiser man than Athanasius, while he regretted Constantius's occasional heterodoxy, praised him for his devotion to the Church. Gregory of Nazianzus, *Oratio IV, Contra Julianum*, in Migne, *Patrologia Graeco-Latina*, XXXV, col. 564.

5 For Julian's opinions and the Christian reaction see Dvornik, *Early Christian and Byzantine Philosophy*, II, pp. 659–86.

6 See *ibid.* vol. II, pp. 731–42.

7 *Codex Theodosianus*, XVI, i, 2, ed. T. Mommsen, P. M. Meyer and others (Berlin, 1905), p. 833.

8 For a full account of the Council, see Hefele–Leclercq, II, i, pp. 1–40. See also G. Bardy and J. R. Palanque, 'La Victoire de l'Orthodoxie', in Fliche and Martin, *Histoire de l'Église*, III, pp. 285–96.

9 See J. R. Palanque, 'L'Expansion Chrétienne', in Fliche and Martin, *Histoire de l'Église*, III, pp. 496–500.

10 See G. Bardy, 'Le Déclin de l'Arianisme', in *ibid*. pp. 263–76; Dvornik, *Early Christian and Byzantine Philosophy*, II, pp. 688–92.

11 Ambrose, *Epistolae*, in Migne, *Patrologia Latina*, XVI, col. 1041.

12 *Ibid*. col. 1152.

13 *Ibid*. col. 1211. Dvornik, *Early Christian and Byzantine Philosophy*, II, pp. 784–5.

14 See J. R. Palanque, *Saint Ambroise et l'Empire Romain* (Paris, 1933), pp. 518 ff.

15 J. R. Palanque, 'Les Métropoles Ecclésiastiques à la fin du IVe siècle', in Fliche and Martin, *Histoire de l'Église*, III, pp. 437–88.

16 L. Bréhier, *Le Monde Byzantin*, II (Paris, 1949), pp. 447–9. See also B. Labanca, 'Del nome Papa nelle chiese cristiane di Oriente ed Occidente', in *Actes du XIIe Congrès Internationale des Orientalistes* (Rome, 1899), III (Florence, 1903), pp. 47 ff.

17 *Codex Theodosianus*, XVI, i, 3, p. 834.

18 For the reign of Arcadius, see J. B. Bury, *History of the Later Roman Empire* (London, 1923), I, pp. 106 ff.; Stein, *Histoire du Bas-Empire*, I, pp. 225 ff.

19 Bury, *History*, p. 138. For the title of Augusta see S. Runciman, 'Some notes on the role of the Empress', *Eastern Churches Review*, IV, 2 (Oxford, 1972), pp. 119–24.

20 Bury, *History*, I, pp. 138 ff.; Stein, *Histoire du Bas-Empire*, I, pp. 241 ff.

21 See Dvornik, *Early Christian and Byzantine Philosophy*, II, pp. 692–9, 785–6.

22 For the whole history of the Monophysite movement up till the final separation of the Monophysite churches see W. H. C. Frend, *The Rise of the Monophysite Movement*

(Cambridge, 1972); for Nestorius in particular, see pp. 16 ff.
See also Bury, *History*, I, pp. 351 ff. and Stein, *Histoire du Bas-Empire*, I, pp. 300 ff. Nestorius's letter to the Emperor is quoted by Socrates, *Historia Ecclesiastica*, in Migne, *Patrologia Graeco-Latina*, LXVII, col. 804.

23 Cyril of Alexandria, *Opera: Apologia ad Theodosium Imperatorem*, in Migne, *Patrologia Graeco-Latina*, LXXVI, coll. 453 ff., esp. col. 458.

24 Frend, *Rise of the Monophysite Movement*, pp. 16–23. For Nestorius's account of the Council of Ephesus – 'Cyril presided; Cyril was accuser; Cyril was judge; Cyril was Bishop of Rome; Cyril was everything' – see Nestorius, *Le Livre d'Héraclide de Damas*, ed. and trans. by F. Nau (Paris, 1910), p. 117. For Pulcheria's quarrel with Nestorius, see *ibid.* p. 89 and the appendix, pp. 363–4 – he had questioned her virginity. For a list of Cyril's bribes, see *ibid.* p. 368.

25 Frend, *Rise of the Monophysite Movement*, pp. 29–33, an excellent and well-referenced account.

26 See Runciman, 'Some notes on the role of the Empress', pp. 120 ff.

27 Frend, *Rise of the Monophysite Movement*, pp. 45–50. For the canons of the Council of Chalcedon, see *Acta Conciliorum Oecumenicorum*, ed. E. Schwartz (4 tomes in 13, Strasbourg, Berlin and Leipzig, 1914–40), II, 1, pp. 80 ff.

28 Frend, *Rise of the Monophysite Movement*, pp. 153–6.

29 See A. S. Atiya, *A History of Eastern Christianity* (London, 1968), pp. 251 ff.

30 Frend, *Rise of the Monophysite Movement*, pp. 157–65; Dvornik, *Early Christian and Byzantine Philosophy*, II, pp. 795–8.

31 *Epistolae Romanorum Pontificum Genuinae*, ed. A. Thiel (Braunsberg, 1867–8), II, p. 203.

32 Evagrius, *Historia Ecclesiastica*, III, 4, ed. H. Valesius (Oxford, 1844), pp. 72–4; Zachariah of Mitylene, *Syriac*

Chronicle, V, 1–4, trans. by F. J. Hamilton and E. W. Brooks (London, 1899), pp. 103–12.

33 Evagrius, *Historia*, ed. Valesius, III, 14, pp. 80–2; Zachariah of Mitylene, *Syriac Chronicle*, V, 8, pp. 121–3. See Frend, *Rise of the Monophysite Movement*, pp. 169–83.

34 See Bury, *History*, I, pp. 429–32.

35 *Ibid.* pp. 432 ff.; Frend, *Rise of the Monophysite Movement*, pp. 184–220.

36 Bury, *History*, II, pp. 405–11.

37 Dvornik, *Early Christian and Byzantine Philosophy*, II, pp. 803–12; Frend, *Rise of the Monophysite Movement*, pp. 193–7. For an analysis of the Gelasian doctrine see W. Ullmann, *The Growth of Papal Government in the Middle Ages* (London, 1955), pp. 14–20.

38 Dvornik, *Early Christian and Byzantine Philosophy*, II, pp. 811–14.

39 For Justin I's religious policy see A. A. Vasiliev, *Justin the First* (Cambridge, Mass., 1950), pp. 132–253.

40 Justinian, *Novellae* (*Corpus Juris Civilis*, ed. R. Schoell and W. Kroll, III, Berlin, 1928), VI, preface IV, pp. 35 ff., also pp. 16, 58, 253; and *Digesta* (*ibid.* vol. I, ed. T. Mommsen and P. Krueger, Berlin, 1928).

41 Frend, *Rise of the Monophysite Movement*, pp. 245–6, 266–9.

42 Bury, *History*, II, pp. 376–7.

43 *Ibid.* vol. II, pp. 377–8; Frend, *Rise of the Monophysite Movement*, pp. 269–73.

44 Frend, *Rise of the Monophysite Movement*, pp. 276–80; Bury, *History*, II, pp. 378–80.

45 Bury, *History*, II, pp. 380–91; Frend, *Rise of the Monophysite Movement*, pp. 280–2.

46 Frend, *Rise of the Monophysite Movement*, pp. 285–7, 318–20.

47 Bury, *History*, II, p. 393.

48 Dvornik, *Early Christian and Byzantine Philosophy*, II, pp. 840–7.

CHAPTER 3 THE BATTLE OVER IMAGES

1 Frend, *Rise of the Monophysite Movement*, pp. 319–22. The text of the *Programma* is given in Evagrius, *Historia*, ed. Valesius, V, 4, pp. 146–9. For a history of these years from a Monophysite point of view, see Michael the Syrian, *Chronicle*, ed. J. B. Chabot (Paris, 1899–1910), II, pp. 294 ff.

2 Frend, *Rise of the Monophysite Movement*, pp. 322–3. Tiberius was popular with the Monophysites because of his tax-reductions. John of Ephesus excuses his persecutions on the ground that he was distracted by the war; John of Ephesus, *Historiae Ecclesiasticae Pars Tertia*, ed. and trans. by R. Payne Smith (Oxford, 1860), pp. 200–4. The Coptic writer, John of Nikiou, in *Chronicle*, ed. and trans. by R. H. Charles (London, 1916), pp. 150–1, calls Tiberius a very good man who put an end to persecution.

3 For the title of 'Oecumenical' see F. Dvornik, *Byzance et la Primauté romaine* (Paris, 1964), pp. 70–2, explaining the true meaning of the title but rather playing down Gregory's indignation.

4 Gregory I, *Epistulae*, in Migne, *Patrologia Latina*, LXXVII, coll. 746–7, 1281–2.

5 For the reign of Phocas see J. B. Bury, *History of the Later Roman Empire from Arcadius to Irene* (London, 1889), II, pp. 197–206, and L. Bréhier, 'L'Empereur Phocas et l'Église', in Fliche and Martin, *Histoire de l'Église*, II, pp. 69–77.

6 Bury, *History...from Arcadius to Irene*, II, pp. 207–26; A. Stratos, *Byzantium in the Seventh Century* (in Greek; Athens, 1966), I, 1, pp. 248 ff.

7 Frend, *Rise of the Monophysite Movement*, pp. 343–51, an account sympathetic to the Monergist doctrine; Bréhier, 'La crise de l'Empire et le redressement d'Héraclius', in

Fliche and Martin, *Histoire de l'Église*, II, 85–90, and 'La nouvelle crise religieuse', in *ibid.* pp. 103–24.

8 Bréhier, 'L'Ekthesis, la fin du règne et la succession d'Héraclius', in *ibid.* pp. 131–4.

9 For the Arab invasions see Stratos, *Byzantium in the Seventh Century*, III (Athens, 1969), *passim*, and A. J. Butler, *The Arab Conquest of Egypt* (London, 1902), *passim*.

10 Bréhier, 'L'Ekthesis', pp. 138–41. For the legal position of the Christians under Arab domination, see A. S. Tritton, *The Caliphs and their Non-Moslem Subjects* (London, 1930), *passim*.

11 See pp. 106–8, 127.

12 See S. Runciman, 'The Byzantine "Protectorate" in the Holy Land', *Byzantion*, XVIII (Brussels, 1948), pp. 207–15.

13 See pp. 106–8, 137.

14 Bréhier, 'Le Démembrement des Chrétientés Orientales', in Fliche and Martin, *Histoire de l'Église*, pp. 160–79.

15 Bréhier, 'Les Derniers Héraclides', in *ibid.* pp. 183–91; Hefele–Leclercq, III, 1, pp. 483 ff.

16 Bréhier, 'Les Derniers Héraclides', pp. 191–200; Hefele–Leclercq, III, 1, pp. 560–81.

17 Bréhier, 'Les Derniers Héraclides', pp. 205–9; Bury, *History...Arcadius to Irene*, II, pp. 363–86.

18 Bury, *History...Arcadius to Irene*, II, pp. 401–7; R. J. H. Jenkins, *Byzantium: The Imperial Centuries* (London, 1966), pp. 58–65.

19 Bury, *History...Arcadius to Irene*, II, pp. 408–24. For the history of the theme system, see *ibid.* pp. 339–51, and G. Ostrogorsky, *History of the Byzantine State*, trans. by J. Hussey (Oxford, 1956), pp. 89–90, 139–40. For the maritime law, see W. Ashburner, *The Rhodian Sea Law* (Oxford, 1909). For the farmer's law and its dating and development, see Ostrogorsky, *History of the Byzantine State*, pp. 120–1, 140.

20 *A Manual of Roman Law: The Ecloga*, ed. and trans. by
    E. H. Freshfield (Cambridge, 1926), esp. pp. 66–70.

21 Ostrogorsky, *History of the Byzantine State*, p. 137,
    note 2.

22 See P. J. Alexander, *The Patriarch Nicephorus of Constanti-
    nople* (Oxford, 1958), pp. 43–4, quoting and commenting
    on Eusebius's letter, which is published in Migne, *Patro-
    logia Graeco-Latina*, xx, coll. 1545–50.

23 For Epiphanius see N. H. Baynes, 'Idolatry and the early
    Church', in Baynes, *Byzantine Studies and Other Essays*,
    pp. 126–8.

24 Baynes, 'Idolatry and the Early Church', p. 136. St Basil's
    words are quoted and amplified by John of Damascus.

25 Leontius of Neapolis, *Sermon against the Jews*, in Migne,
    Patrolgia Graeco-Latina, xciii, coll. 1604 ff.

26 For the whole question see Baynes, 'Idolatry and the early
    Church', pp. 116 ff.; Ostrogorsky, *Studien zur Geschichte
    des byzantinischen Bilderstreites* (Breslau, 1929); E. Kitzinger,
    'The Cult of Images before Iconoclasm', in *Dumbarton Oaks
    Papers*, viii (Cambridge, Mass., 1954), pp. 85–150.

27 See Kitzinger, 'Cult of images', pp. 100 ff.

28 Baynes, 'The supernatural defenders of Constantinople', in
    Baynes, *Byzantine Studies and Other Essays*, pp. 248 ff.

29 Canon 82 of the Quinisext Council, in Mansi, *Concilia*, xi,
    coll. 977–80.

30 See note 39.

31 A. Grabar, *L'Iconoclasme Byzantin: dossier archéologique*
    (Paris, 1957), pp. 39–45.

32 *Ibid.* pp. 77–91.

33 *Ibid.* pp. 94–9; Kitzinger, 'Cult of images', pp. 129–34.
    Arculf's experience is given in his *Relatio de Locis Sanctis*,
    iii, 4, in T. Tobler, *Itinera Hierosolymitana et Descriptiones
    Terrae Sanctae* (Geneva, 1879–85), p. 200. Arculf believed
    the attacker to be a Jew.

34 See P. Alexander, 'An Ascetic Sect of Iconoclasts in seventh-century Armenia', in *Studies in Honor of Albert Matthias Friend* (Princeton, 1953), pp. 151–60.

35 Grabar, *L'Iconoclasme*, pp. 105–12, with a commentary on Yezid's decree.

36 Theophanes, *Chronographia*, ed. C. de Boor (Leipzig, 1883), p. 402. Letters of the Patriarch Germanus in Mansi, *Concilia*, pp. 99–105, 105–7, 107–27.

37 Theophanes, *Chronographia*, p. 402. The story of Sarantapechys was told to the Oecumenical Council of Nicaea in 787 by a monk John who represented the Patriarch of Jerusalem. The text of his statement is given in Mansi, *Concilia*, XIII, coll. 196–200, and in Migne, *Patrologia Graeco-Latina*, CIX, coll. 517–20.

38 Theophanes, *Chronographia*, pp. 404–5; Nicephorus Patriarcha, *Opuscula Historica*, ed. de Boor (Leipzig, 1880), p. 59.

39 Theophanes, *Chronographia*, p. 405; *Vita Sancti Stephani Junioris*, in Migne, *Patrologia Graeco-Latina*, C, col. 1085. For a discussion of the event and the legends that grew up around it, see Grabar, *L'Iconoclasme*, pp. 130 ff.

40 Theophanes, *Chronographia*, p. 405. Nicephorus, *Opuscula Historica*, pp. 57–8.

41 Theophanes, *Chronographia*, p. 405. The story told later by George the Monk (*Chronicon*, ed. de Boor [Leipzig, 1904], II, p. 742), and repeated much later by Zonaras (*Synopsis Historiarum*, III [Bonn edn, 1897], p. 340), which tells of Leo burning down an Imperial academy for theology and the arts, with its professors and books inside, is obviously a subsequent embellishment. See Bury, *History...Arcadius to Irene*, II, pp. 433–4.

42 Theophanes, *Chronographia*, pp. 407–8; *Le Liber Pontificalis*, ed. L. Duchesne (Paris, 1886–92), I, p. 404. For the authenticity of the Pope's letters, which have survived only in a Greek translation (given in Mansi, *Concilia*, XII, coll.

959 ff.), see Ostrogorsky, *History of the Byzantine State*, pp. 133–4.

43 Theophanes, *Chronographia*, pp. 408–9; Nicephorus, *Opuscula Historica*, p. 58.

44 Theophanes, *Chronographia*, p. 409. For the dating of the sequence of events, see Ostrogorsky, 'Les Débuts de la querelle des images', in *Mélanges Charles Diehl* (Paris, 1930), I, pp. 235–55.

45 Bury, *History...Arcadius to Irene*, II, pp. 439–49; Ostrogorsky, *History of the Byzantine State*, pp. 145–7. See also V. Grumel, 'L'Annexion de l'Illyricum oriental, de la Sicile et de la Calabre au Patriarchat de Constantinople', in *Recherches de Science Réligieuse*, XL (Paris, 1952), pp. 191–200.

46 Bury, *History...Arcadius to Irene*, II, p. 433.

47 For a summary of Constantine V's earlier years see Ostrogorsky, *History of the Byzantine State*, pp. 147–52.

48 For the transportation of populations see Theophanes, *Chronographia*, pp. 422, 423, 429; Nicephorus, *Opuscula Historica*, pp. 62–3, 65–6.

49 For Constantine's character see Bury, *History...Arcadius to Irene*, II, pp. 460–2; Bréhier, 'La Querelle des images', in Fliche and Martin, *Histoire de l'Église*, III, pp. 457–8. His views on the Virgin and the Saints are reported in John of Damascus, *Adversus Constantinum Caballinum*; Migne, *Patrologia Graeco-Latina*, XCV, col. 337 (a spurious work, for which see Alexander, *The Patriarch Nicephorus*, pp. 234–5); and the ninth-century *Vita Nicetae Mediciensis*, in *Acta Sanctorum*, April, I, p. 260. Of his Paulician connections it is only possible to say that the Paulicians suffered no persecution in his time, and that he may have met the Paulician leader Gegnesius, who visited Constantinople in Leo III's reign. See S. Runciman, *The Medieval Manichee* (Cambridge, 1947), pp. 38–9, 183.

50 See H. Leclercq, 'Jean Damascène', *Dictionnaire d'Arché-*

ologie Chrétienne, VII, coll. 2186–90; Alexander, *Patriarch Nicephorus*, pp. 49–50, 199–200. For Leo's words, 'I am priest and king', see Mansi, *Concilia*, XII, col. 976.

51 See Ostrogorsky, *Studien zur Geschichte des byzantinischen Bilderstreites*, pp. 14–15.

52 For the Council of 754 see Bréhier, La Querelle des images', pp. 468–71, and for a detailed discussion of its theology, M. V. Anastos, 'The argument for Iconoclasm as presented by the Iconoclastic Council of 754', in *Studies in Honor of A. M. Friend*, pp. 177 ff.

53 Bury, *History...Arcadius to Irene*, II, p. 463.

54 *Ibid.* pp. 463–6.

55 *Ibid.* pp. 469 ff.

56 Ostrogorsky, *History of the Byzantine State*, pp. 151–2.

57 Bury, *History...Arcadius to Irene*, II, pp. 477–9.

CHAPTER 4   THE WORKING COMPROMISE

1 The eighth-century Iconoclasts talked of the time when 'the Empire was transferred from men to a woman and the Church was ruined by womanly simplicity', words quoted and challenged by the Patriarch Nicephorus in his *Refutatio et Eversio*, summarized from an unpublished text in Alexander, *The Patriarch Nicephorus*, pp. 247–8.

2 Theophanes, *Chronographia*, pp. 457–8; Nicephorus, *Refutatio*, in Alexander, *The Patriarch Nicephorus*, pp. 247–8.

3 Theophanes, *Chronographia*, pp. 458–60. See I. Andreev, *Germanus and Tarasius, Patriarchs of Constantinople* (in Russian; Sergiev Posad, 1907), p. 98.

4 Theophanes, *Chronographia*, pp. 460–1. Hadrian's letter is given in Mansi, *Concilia*, XII, coll. 1056–7. Hadrian was distressed because Tarasius was not only a layman but had been a soldier.

5 See Alexander, *The Patriarch Nicephorus*, pp. 18–20, with references, for the events preceding the Council.

6 The Acts of the Council are given in Mansi, *Concilia*, XII and XIII. For the operative clause, see Mansi, XIII, coll. 3770–2. For the Pope's reaction, see Alexander, *The Patriarch Nicephorus*, pp. 104–5.

7 The monks' disapproval of the clemency of the authorities is shown in Theodore of Studium, *Epistulae*, in Migne, *Patrologia Graeco-Latina*, XCIX, col. 1044. Their spokesman was Sabas of Studion.

8 P. and J. Zepos, *Jus Graecoromanum* (Athens, 1931), I, p. 45, cite two laws of Irene's in which she is called the 'pious Emperor'.

9 For the Moechian Controversy, see Alexander, *The Patriarch Nicephorus*, pp. 82 ff.

10 Bury, *History...Arcadius to Irene*, pp. 491–2. For Irene's treaties with the Saracens, see F. Dölger, *Regesten der Kaiserurkunden des oströmischen Reiches*, I (Munich–Berlin, 1924), Reg. 340, 352, pp. 42, 43.

11 Ostrogorsky, *History of the Byzantine State*, pp. 162–5; Jenkins, *Byzantium*, pp. 105–16.

12 Theophanes, *Chronographia*, pp. 475–7.

13 For the reign and reforms of Nicephorus, see Ostrogorsky, *History of the Byzantine State*, pp. 166–73. For his actions over the Moechian controversy, see Alexander, *The Patriarch Nicephorus*, pp. 85–9.

14 The accusation of heterodoxy comes from Theophanes (*Chronographia*, pp. 476–80), who detested Nicephorus, and should perhaps be discounted. See Alexander, *The Patriarch Nicephorus*, pp. 72–3.

15 Ostrogorsky, *History of the Byzantine State*, pp. 173–5.

16 For the confrontations between the Patriarch and Theodore of Studion, see the fully referenced account in Alexander,

The Patriarch Nicephorus, pp. 99–101, an account that is perhaps a little unfair to Theodore.

17 Ostrogorsky, *History of the Byzantine State*, pp. 177–8; Alexander, *The Patriarch Nicephorus*, pp. 77–8.

18 Alexander, *The Patriarch Nicephorus*, pp. 125–32, with references.

19 *Ibid.* pp. 134–5.

20 Theodore of Studion, *Epistulae*, col. 1417.

21 *Ibid.* col. 1001.

22 Alexander, *The Patriarch Nicephorus*, pp. 137–40.

23 *Ibid.* pp. 140–7; Theodore of Studion, *Epistulae*, col. 1305.

24 Bury, *A History of the Eastern Roman Empire* (London, 1912), pp. 110–19.

25 See B. von Simson, *Jahrbücher des fränkishen Reichs unter Ludwig dem Frommen* (Leipzig, 1874–6), I, pp. 248 ff.

26 Bury, *Eastern Roman Empire*, pp. 110–11.

27 For the reign of Theophilus see Bury, *Eastern Roman Empire*, pp. 120 ff.; Ostrogorsky, *History of the Byzantine State*, pp. 183–6; Jenkins, *Byzantium*, pp. 146–52. For his buildings, see Grabar, *L'Iconoclasme Byzantin*, pp. 142 ff.

28 See G. Mathew, *Byzantine Aesthetics* (London, 1963), pp. 122 ff.

29 Bury, *Eastern Roman Empire*, pp. 143–53.

30 The standard work on the whole story of Ignatius and Photius is F. Dvornik, *The Photian Schism* (Cambridge, 1948). But Dvornik is a little over-anxious to prove that Photius bore no hostility towards Rome. The account in Jenkins, *Byzantium*, pp. 168–81, is better balanced, but lacks references. The account in Bury, *Eastern Roman Empire*, pp. 180–209, is still valuable.

31 Dvornik, *Photian Schism*, pp. 39 ff.; Bury, *Eastern Roman Empire*, pp. 161 ff. H. Grégoire in several articles, especially 'Études sur le neuvième siècle', *Byzantion*, VIII (Brussels, 1933), pp. 515 ff., attempts to rehabilitate Michael III,

showing that he was the victim of later hostile propaganda, but somewhat overstates his case. See Jenkins, *Byzantium*, pp. 156–7.

32 Dvornik, *Photian Schism*, pp. 132 ff.; Bury, *Eastern Roman Empire*, pp. 165–79.

33 The text of the *Epanagoge* is given in Zepos, *Jus Graecoromanum*, II, pp. 236–368. Titulus III deals with the Patriarch. On the question of its publication see Ostrogorsky, *History of the Byzantine State*, p. 213, note 2.

34 Ostrogorsky, *History of the Byzantine State*, pp. 214–15; Jenkins, *Byzantium*, pp. 200 ff. For the correct dating and Stephen's age (19, not 16, as Ostrogorsky says), see Jenkins, 'The chronological accuracy of the "Logothete" for the years A.D. 867–913', in *Dumbarton Oaks Papers*, XIX (Cambridge, Mass., 1965), pp. 98–100. The monkish author of the *Vita Ignatii* (in Migne, *Patrologia Graeco-Latina*, CV, col. 573) alludes to Stephen as a 'make-believe' Patriarch, not because of his youth or his rank, but because he had been ordained by Photius.

35 For this synod see Dvornik, *Photian Schism*, pp. 265 ff., casting certain doubts on it.

36 See Jenkins, 'A note on the Patriarch Nicholas Mysticus', in *Acta Antiqua Academiae Scientiarum Hungaricae*, II (Budapest, 1963), pp. 145–7, showing that Nicholas was not Photius's nephew, as Dvornik (*Photian Schism*, pp. 248–9) and others maintain, but had been a slave in his household.

37 Basil of Caesarea, Canon IV, in Migne, *Patrologia Graeco-Latina*.

38 Leo VI, *Novellae*, 90, in Zepos, *Jus Graecoromanum*, I, pp. 156–7.

39 Jenkins, *Byzantium*, pp. 200, 202, 214. The name 'Zaoutzes' is clearly derived from the Armenian word 'zaoutch', meaning a negro.

40 Jenkins, *Byzantium*, pp. 212–14.

41 *Ibid.* pp. 214–26, the best recent account of the affair, based not only on Theophanes Continuatus and other chroniclers but on the letters of Arethas, which throw a fresh light on the story. See Jenkins, 'Eight letters of Arethas', in *Hellenika*, xiv (Thessalonica, 1956), pp. 293–372, also 'Three documents concerning the "Tetragamy"', in *Dumbarton Oaks Papers*, xvi (Cambridge, Mass., 1962), pp. 231–41.

42 Jenkins, *Byzantium*, pp. 227–31; Runciman, *The Emperor Romanus Lecapenus* (Cambridge, 1929), pp. 45–53.

43 Runciman, *Romanus Lecapenus*, pp. 52–62.

44 Jenkins, *Byzantium*, pp. 237–8. The text of the *tomus* is given in V. Grumel, *Les Regestes des Actes du Patriarchat de Constantinople*, *I*, *Les Actes des Patriarcat*, Reg. 669.

45 Jenkins, *Byzantium*, pp. 252–3; Runciman, *Romanus Lecapenus*, pp. 75–7.

46 Jenkins, *Byzantium*, pp. 253, 266–7.

47 *Ibid.* pp. 277–8.

48 Zonaras, *Synopsis Historiarum*, iii, p. 509.

49 Leo Diaconus, *Historia* (Bonn edn, 1828), pp. 98–9. See also Ostrogorsky, *History of the Byzantine State*, p. 260, note 2.

50 Leo Diaconus, *Historia*, pp. 101–2.

51 See Jenkins, *Byzantium*, pp. 308–9, 320, 329–31.

52 Michael Attaliates, *Historia* (Bonn edn, 1853).

53 See Runciman, *The Eastern Schism* (Oxford, 1955), pp. 28–54.

54 Attaliates, *Historia*, p. 60; *Cedrenus-Scylitzes* (Bonn edn, 1838), ii, pp. 641–4. Ostrogorsky, *History of the Byzantine State*, pp. 301–2, is, I think, wrong in associating the Emperor Isaac's abdication with unpopularity because of his treatment of the Patriarch: whose fall seems, according to the sources, to have caused no stir. The account given by Psellus (*Chronographia*, ed. and trans. by E. Renaud

[Paris, 1928], II, p. 123) is very equivocal. Psellus himself was almost certainly involved in a plot against the Emperor.

CHAPTER 5   THE MONKS AND THE PEOPLE

1 Byzantine disquisitions on kingship all insist that the monarch should be dignified and detached, while remaining humble and charitable, e.g. Photius, *Letter to Michael (Boris), Prince of Bulgaria*, in Migne, *Patrologia Graeco-Latina*, CII, coll. 627–96, or Nicephorus Blemmydas, *The Statue of a King* (as re-written by a deacon of St Sophia, *c.* 1300), in A. Mai, *Scriptorum Veterum Nova Collectio*, II (Rome, 1828), coll. 609–70.

2 Theophanes Continuatus (Bonn edn, 1838), pp. 199–200.

3 See L. Bréhier, *Le Monde Byzantin*, II, *Les Institutions de l'Empire Byzantin* (Paris, 1949), p. 434.

4 See p. 73.

5 See p. 144.

6 Bréhier, *Le Monde Byzantin*, pp. 529 ff.

7 *Ibid.* pp. 533 ff.

8 Justinian, *Novellae*, ed. K. E. Zachariae von Lingenthal (Leipzig, 1881), I, pp. 133, 535, 538, 539, 554. See Bréhier, *Le Monde Byzantin*, pp. 550 ff.

9 Bréhier, *Le Monde Byzantin*, pp. 545–6.

10 *Ibid.* pp. 536, 557–8.

11 See pp. 78–9, 93. Most of the eminent Patriarchs of the ninth and tenth centuries were laymen up till the time of their appointment (e.g. Tarasius, Photius, Nicholas Mysticus), though later nearly every Patriarch had already taken priestly, but not necessarily monastic, vows.

12 Bréhier, *Le Monde Byzantin*, pp. 513–14.

13 The ninth-century Emperors Leo V, Michael II and Basil I were all of humble origin, Basil I being illiterate. The

historian Psellus, though he claimed noble descent, was the son of a small shop-keeper, and his mother, left a poor widow, taught herself to read in order to educate her son.

14 For example, Ignatius was the son of a fallen Emperor, Stephen the brother of a reigning Emperor, and Photius came of a noble family, but Nicetas was the son of a Slav immigrant, Polyeuct was apparently of humble birth, and Nicholas Mysticus the son of a slave-woman.

15 See p. 47.

16 See H. Delehaye, *Les Saints Stylites* (Brussels–Paris, 1923), pp. i–xxxix, 1–147 (life of St Daniel), 148–94 (life of St Alypius). St Theodulus is mentioned in a letter written by Theodore of Studion (see Migne, *Patrologia Graeco-Latina*, IC, col. 957). For the female Stylites see note by Delehaye in *Analecta Bollandiana*, XXVII (Brussels, 1908), pp. 391–2.

17 For the life of St Luke the Stylite, see Delehaye, *Les Saints Stylites*, pp. 195–237. The life of St Basil the Less is given in *Acta Sanctorum*, 26 Mart., III, pp. 668–81. The life of Holy Luke is given in Migne, *Patrologia Graeco-Latina*, CXI, coll. 465 ff.

18 For Gregory of Sinai see B. Tatakis, *La Philosophie Byzantine* (Paris, 1949), pp. 261–3; V. Losky, *The Mystical theology of the Eastern Church* (London, 1957), pp. 209–10.

19 For the foundation of the monastery of St Symeon (Kaalat Seman), see Grabar, *Martyrium* (Paris, 1946), I, pp. 156–7, 364–5. For the foundation of Holy Luke, see C. Diehl, *L'Église et les Mosaïques du Couvent de Saint-Luc en Phocide* (Paris, 1889), pp. 8–21.

20 See p. 76.

21 See p. 81. For Plato see A. Gardner, *Theodore of Studium* (London, 1905), pp. 16, 25–6, 31 ff.

22 For Theodore, see Gardner, *Theodore of Studium*, and E. Amann, 'Théodore le Studite', *Dictionnaire de Théologie Catholique*, XV, i, coll. 287–98. For a summary of his

monastic reforms, see Bréhier, *Le Monde Byzantin*, II, pp. 540–4.

23 See pp. 82, 84.

24 For the anecdote about Photius and Ignatius, see Bury, *Eastern Roman Empire*, p. 187. On the other hand the Patriarch Polyeuct was, according to Leo Diaconus (p. 32), 'learned in human and divine philosophy'.

25 Public opinion in Byzantium was certainly affected by the creation in the West of a 'Roman' Empire which did not recognize the Byzantine Emperor as Roman Emperor, from the time of Otto I onwards. The Carolingians had regarded the Byzantine sovereigns as co-Emperors. See Jenkins, *Byzantium*, pp. 353–4.

26 See p. 108.

27 Bréhier, *Le Monde Byzantin*, II, pp. 553 ff.

28 Ostrogorsky, *History of the Byzantine State*, pp. 254–7.

29 See p. 103.

30 Ostrogorsky, *History of the Byzantine State*, pp. 271–2; Jenkins, *Byzantium*, pp. 319–20.

31 See J. Gouillard, 'Syméon le Jeune', *Dictionnaire de Théologie Catholique*, XIV, 2, coll. 2941–56.

32 There is no adequate historical study of the monasteries of Constantinople. Historians have tended to concentrate upon the rural monasteries. But see J. M. Hussey, *Church and Learning in the Byzantine Empire* (London, 1937), pp. 183–9.

33 For the destruction of monasteries in Asia Minor see S. Vryonis, *The Decline of Medieval Hellenism in Asia Minor* (Univ. California, 1971), esp. pp. 194–7. For scandals on Mount Athos, when Constantine IX had already been obliged to set up a commission to inquire into scandals in 1052, see P. Meyer, *Die Haupturkunden der Athos-Klöster* (Leipzig, 1894), pp. 158–84.

34 Anna Comnena, *Alexiade*, ed. and trans. by B. Leib (Paris, 1937), I, pp. 103–10. Anna is clearly a little disingenuous

about her parents' troubles. See F. Chalandon, *Essai sur le Règne d'Alexis 1er Comnène* (Paris, 1900), pp. 53–6.

35 Bréhier, *Le Monde Byzantin*, II, pp. 556–7: Hussey, *Church and Learning*, pp. 175–7; Chalandon, *Essai*, pp. 282–7. For Eustathius's views, see his *De Emendata Vita Monachica*, in Migne, *Patrologia Graeco-Latina*, CXXXV, col. 749.

36 Benjamin of Tudela, *Itinerary*, trans. by M. N. Adler (London, 1907), pp. 11–14.

37 Chalandon, *Les Comnène, II, Jean II Comnène et Manuel I Comnène* (Paris, 1912), pp. 627–33.

38 D. Obolensky, *The Bogomils* (Cambridge, 1948), pp. 168 ff.; Runciman, *The Medieval Manichee*, pp. 70 ff.

39 Runciman, 'The end of Anna Dalassena', *Mélanges Henri Grégoire*, I (Brussels, 1949), pp. 517–25.

40 Comnena, *Alexiade* III, pp. 218–28.

41 John Cinnamus, *Historia* (Bonn edn, 1836), p. 65. Chalandon, *Les Comnène*, pp. 636–9.

42 Runciman, *The Eastern Schism*, pp. 78 ff.; W. Norden, *Das Papsttum und Byzanz* (Berlin, 1903), pp. 59 ff.

43 Chalandon, *Les Comnène*, pp. 643–7, 660–3.

44 Nicetas Choniates, *Historia* (Bonn edn, 1835), pp. 430–1.

CHAPTER 6   DECLINE AND FALL

1 For a general summary of the period see Ostrogorsky, *History of the Byzantine State*, pp. 311 ff.

2 The change in style can first be seen in the mosaics in the church at Daphne, near Athens, decorated probably about 1175. See F. Diez and O. Demus, *Byzantine Churches in Greece* (Cambridge, Mass., 1931), pp. 91 ff. It can be seen at its most poignant in the small church at Nerez, in Macedonia, commissioned by a Byzantine prince in 1164. See A. Grabar, *Byzantine Painting* (London, 1953), pp. 141–3.

3 Ostrogorsky, *History of the Byzantine State*, esp. pp. 358 ff.

4 *Ibid.* pp. 365–70.

5 *Ibid.* pp. 375–80.

6 See Runciman, *The Eastern Schism*, pp. 154–6, with references.

7 Ostrogorsky, *History of the Byzantine State*, pp. 379–80; A. Gardner, *The Lascarids of Nicaea* (London, 1912), pp. 7–8, 97–8.

8 See Archbishop Chrysanthos, *The Church of Trebizond* (in Greek; Athens, 1933), pp. 177–8; A. D. Karpozilos, *The Ecclesiastical Controversy between the Kingdom of Nicaea and the Principality of Epiros* (Thessalonica, 1973), *passim*.

9 Theodore Balsamon, *Meditata*, in Migne, *Patrologia Graeco-Latina*, cxxxviii, coll. 1017–20. Demetrius Chomatianus, letter, in J. B. Pitra, *Analecta Sacra et Classica* (Paris–Rome, 1891), coll. 473–8.

10 Gardner, *The Lascarids*, pp. 94–5, 112–13.

11 *Ibid.* pp. 168 ff.

12 *Ibid.* pp. 169–71, with references, and pp. 300–1, reproducing Blemmydas's own account.

13 *Ibid.* pp. 171, 198, 206–8, with references.

14 Nicephorus Blemmydas, *Oratio de Regis Officiis*, in Migne, *Patrologia Graeco-Latina*, cxlii, coll. 612 ff. The work exists in two forms, the second being a re-edition by a monk of the next century.

15 For the youth of Michael Palaeologus and his rise to power the best modern account is in D. J. Geanakoplos, *Emperor Michael Palaeologus and the West* (Cambridge, Mass., 1959), pp. 16–46. There are various discrepancies in the chief sources, Acropolita and Pachymer, who were contemporaries, and Gregoras, writing in the next century.

16 *Ibid.* pp. 45–115.

17 George Pachymer, *De Michaele et Andronico Palaeologis* (Bonn edn, 1835), pp. 193–201.

18 See L. Petit, 'Arsène Autorianus et les Arsénites', *Diction-naire de Théologie Catholique*, I, ii, coll. 1991–4; Runciman, *The Great Church in Captivity* (Cambridge, 1968), pp. 66–8.

19 Pachymer, *De Michaele et Andronico Palaeologis*, pp. 257–70, 278–9, 303–9.

20 Petit, 'Arsène Autorianus'; I. E. Troitsky, *Arsenius and the Arsenites* (in Russian; St Petersburg, 1873), esp. pp. 99–101.

21 Geanakoplos, *Emperor Michael Palaeologus*, pp. 189–95, 237–45, 258–9.

22 *Ibid.* pp. 259–76.

23 See D. M. Nicol, *The Last Centuries of Byzantium* (London, 1972), pp. 99–102.

24 *Ibid.* pp. 102–5.

25 *Ibid.* pp. 105–10. See also A. E. Laiou, *Constantinople and the Latins* (Cambridge, Mass., 1972), pp. 32–6, 122–6, 194–6, and R. Guilland, 'La Correspondance inédite d'Athanase, patriarche de Constantinople', *Études Byzantines* (Paris, 1959), pp. 53–79.

26 Nicol, *Last Centuries*, pp. 110–12; Laiou, *Constantinople*, pp. 245–6.

27 Nicol, *Last Centuries*, p. 111.

28 Vryonis, *Decline of Medieval Hellenism*, pp. 288 ff., esp. pp. 303 ff., with texts.

29 Dolger, *Regesten* (Munich–Berlin, 1924–60, in progress), IV, no. 2342, pp. 59–60; P. Meyer, *Die Haupturkunden für die Geschichte der Athos-Klöster* (Leipzig, 1894), pp. 190–4.

30 Philotheus, *Encomium Gregorae Palamae*, in Migne, *Patrologia Graeco-Latina*, CLI, col. 553. The minister was the father of Gregory Palamas.

31 Laiou, *Constantinople*, pp. 308 ff.

32 Nicol, *Last Centuries*, pp. 162–8; U. V. Bosch, *Kaiser Andronikos III Palaeologos* (Amsterdam, 1965), pp. 19–52.

33 Nicol, *Last Centuries*, pp. 172–214; Bosch, *Kaiser Andronikos III Palaeologos*, pp. 67 ff.

34 See J. Meyendorff, *Introduction à l'étude de Grégoire Palamas* (Paris, 1959), *passim*; Runciman, *Great Church in Captivity*, pp. 138–58.

35 See O. Tafrali, *Thessalonique au XIVe siècle* (Paris, 1913), pp. 225–72; P. Charanis, 'Internal strife in Byzantium during the fourteenth century', *Byzantium*, xv (1940–1), pp. 208–30; I. Sevčenko, 'Nicholas Cabasilas' "Anti-Zealot" discourse: a reinterpretation', *Dumbarton Oaks Papers*, xi (1957), pp. 79–171; Meyendorff, *Saint Grégoire Palamas* (Paris, 1959), pp. 111–12.

36 O. Halecki, *Un Empereur de Byzance à Rome* (Warsaw, 1930), pp. 188 ff.

37 V. Laurent, 'Les Droits de l'empereur en matière ecclésiastique. L'accord de 1380–1382', *Revue des Études Byzantines*, xiii (1955), pp. 5–20.

38 The text of the Patriarch's letter is given in F. Miklosich and I. Muller, *Acta et Diplomata Graeca Medii Aevi* (Vienna, 1860–90), ii, pp. 188–92.

39 Laurent, 'Les Droits de l'empereur'; Sylvester Syropoulos, *Memoirs*, ed. and trans. by R. Creyghton (The Hague, 1660), pp. 1–2.

40 Georgios Sphrantzes, *Memorii 1401–1477*, ed. V. Grecu (Bucarest, 1966), p. 320.

41 The fullest account of the Council of Florence is in J. Gill, *The Council of Florence* (Cambridge, 1966). See also Geanakoplos, *Byzantine East and Latin West* (Oxford, 1965), pp. 84–111; Runciman, *Great Church in Captivity*, pp. 105–9.

42 Gill, *Council of Florence*, pp. 354–65; Runciman, *Great Church in Captivity*, pp. 309–11.

43 See Runciman, *The Fall of Constantinople* (Cambridge, 1965), pp. 126–32.

INDEX

Index

Index

Index

Index

Index

Index

Index